IN DEFENCE OF THE SUNNĪ (

CW00937996

Every Innovation is Misguidance

Shaikh Maḥmūd Aḥmad Mirpūrī

[1409H]

Compiled, Translated and Annotated

Abū Ḥibbān Malak

Abū Khuzaimah ʿImrān Masoom Anṣārī

Salafi Research Institute

LONDON - BIRMINGHAM - LAHORE

بِسۡمِ ٱللَّهِ ٱلرَّحۡمَٰنِ ٱلرَّحِيمِ

كل الحقوق محفوظة

Every Innovation is Misguidance
by Shaikh Maḥmūd Aḥmad Mirpūrī (d.1988/1409)
Compiled, Translated & Annotated
by Abū Ḥibbān Malak & Abū Khuzaimah ᶜImrān Masoom Anṣārī

ISBN: 978-0-9954520-0-8
Published by Salafi Research Institute
First Edition: Shaᶜbān 1437 / May 2016
Typeset: Salafi Research Institute
Cover design: Ihsaan Design – www.ihssaandesign.co.uk

Published in conjunction with

MAKTABAH ASHAB AL-HADITH

MAKTABAH AL-IMAM BADI AL-DIN SINDHI

Salafi Research Institute
Suite M0162, 265-269 Kingston Road, Wimbledon, London, SW19 3NW
Web: www.salafiri.com - Email: info@salafiri.com
Tel/Mob: +44 (0)7497 261 845

SALAFI RESEARCH INSTITUTE
LONDON - BIRMINGHAM - LAHORE

فهرس

Contents

مُقَدِّمَة

Introduction

Alḥamdullilāhi Rabbil Acلamīn, Waṣalatu Wasalam Ala Rasūlillahil Karīm, Wa Bacd

It is very difficult to introduce a book written by our teacher, the late esteemed Shaikh, Muhaqqiq, Muftī Mawlāna Maḥmūd Aḥmad Mirpūrī *rahimahullāh* without stepping back into history and remembering the Shaikh, his efforts and struggle against the people of *shirk* and *bidcah.* In this very brief introduction to the Shaikhs book on *bidcah* I would like to mention two noble characteristics that our Shaikh possessed by the grace of Allāh and it is by these qualities that he tried to live his life and exert his efforts in the field of dacwah.

The first of these characteristics is that of the Shaikh submitting and holding on firmly to the book of Allāh, Sunnah of the Messenger of Allāh (ﷺ) and way of the *Salaf* without compromise or being apologetic. The Shaikh in his *cAqīdah* and *Manhaj* walillahilḥamd was Ahl al-Ḥadīth and he openly proclaimed this by way of his words, actions and numerous writings and Fatāwa. Our Shaikh was a very simple man who had great wisdom and love for all of the *Ummah* seeking its rectification upon the correct creed and *Manhaj* of the *Salaf.* Where the Shaikh was gentle with the masses he remained steadfast and fervent in defending the book and the Sunnah not shying away from speaking the truth.

An example of the Shaikhs great wisdom and adherence to the *Manhaj* of the Salaf can be found in the hundreds of Islamic Fatāwa and verdicts that the Shaikh would be frequently asked about by the Ummah of the UK, Europe and beyond. A questioner from Wilbert in Western Germany, Iftikhār Aḥmad asked about the various sects such as the Barailwī's, Deobandī's, Jamāt al-Islāmī, the Qur'ānites and how the laymen can seek which is upon the truth. The Shaikh's response is fairly detailed but we record below some extracts from the Shaikh's response,

"Allāh informs us in the Qur'ān, he says ***"Do not split into sects" [Āle ᶜImrān :103]*** *as this divides the ummah and weakens it. Those sects and groups whom you have mentioned all claim to be the flagbearers of Islām and callers to the Book and Sunnah but we have to establish the validity of this. The problem occurs when a layperson from the masses goes around lending his ear to all these groups and it becomes difficult for him to decide whom he should listen to and whose call he should respond to. But like all other problems the Book and Sunnah have given us a solution to this problem despite the multitude of numerous sects and groups. Allāh says,* ***"O you who believe! Obey Allāh and obey the Messenger and those of you (Muslims) who are in authority. (And) if you differ in anything amongst yourselves, refer it to Allāh and His Messenger if you believe in Allāh and in the Last Day. That is better and more suitable for final determination." [al-Nisā:59]*** *This āyah is clear in establishing that we should obey Allāh, his Messenger and the khalīfah and ruler of a muslim country so long as his sayings do not contravene the religion and in all disputes to refer back to the book and the Sunnah. In situations of dispute one will cannot follow his own desires, opions of others or the majority but he must refer back to the book and the Sunnah.*

So let it be known that the Prophet (ﷺ) warned us about sects and groups, so no matter how large the sect is, and the noble claims that it may make about itself, or the noble names by which it may call itself with all this does not necessarily mean the sect is upon the truth in fact all such sects can be upon misguidance and deviation and the one true group of salvation can only be the one who adheres to the way of the prophet and his companions. So we do not look at the claims and slogans of these sects but look instead at their call and whether it is accordance with the Prophet (ﷺ) and Ṣahābah. It is incumbent in the presence of all these sects that the layperson stays well away from hizbiyyah (partisanship to a particular group/sect), blind following (taqlīd) and the customs and practices of the people and instead adhere to the way of the Book and the Sunnah and Ṣahābah. The group which calls to this specific way of daᶜwah then one should accept its call and cooperate with it.

One should strive to study the Qur'ān with translation, books of Ḥadīth such as Bukhārī, Muslim and others and books of Sīrah and basic ᶜAqīdah and beliefs and in this way a person can get a basic grounding in the religion. As for the Deobandī's and Barailwī's then these sects are from the Indian subcontinent and both are Ḥanafīs and two branches of same tree. Some Deobandī scholars differed with the Barailwī's and in this way two groups emerged evolving into two separate sects.

As for Jamāt al-Islāmī then it is a sect based upon political objectives calling to Islām and has within it people of all sects and groups. As for the Ahl al-Ḥadīth then they call to the pure way which is the book of Allāh, Sunnah of the Prophet (ﷺ) and the Ṣaḥābah. They call people to purify their belief in Tawḥīd of all kinds of major and minor shirk and to accept the Sunnah from all kinds of bidᶜah. They do not blindly follow one Imām or a madhab like Ḥanafī's, Shāfᶜī's, Mālikī's and Hanbalī's do and only accept verdicts of Imāms that are in accordance with the book and Sunnah." End of the Shaikhs words. [*Fatāwa Ṣirāt al-Mustaqīm* [pp.519-522].

We say we learn a lot about our Shaikhs *Manhaj* of adhering to the truth without compromise or hiding the truth and there are many benefits that can be gained about the Shaikh's *Manhaj* from this verdict alone including:

- The simplicity and directness of the Shaikh's daᶜwah.
- His hatred of splitting the ummah into sects and parties
- His mentioning of the names and the founders of deviant sects not hiding behind generalisations or unclear general speech.
- His importance not only to daᶜwah which revolved around a positive call to Tawḥīd and Sunnah but his warning against falling into the opposites of *shirk* and *bidᶜah*, thus, his daᶜwah was not only of affirmation as done by some today but that of the Salaf by way of affirmation and negation.
- His fervour to refute the people of *shirk* and *bidᶜah* and explains their mistakes openly even to the common man so that he does not fall into the error of the misguided sects.
- His adherence to the *Manhaj* of the Salaf in not performing *muwāzanah* (mentioning the good alongside the bad of a deviated sect) or *muḍāhanah* (to renounce or compromise something from the Religion to please those people [kufār or *Ahl al-Bidᶜah*).

- His firmness making the Ahl al-Ḥadīth as a completely distinct and separate way from the innovated and misguided sects.
- His clear call that just to name oneself with Jamīyyah Ahl al-Ḥadīth, Salafī or other than that that with slogans etc is not enough for salvation as this only lies in following the book, Sunnah and way of the Salaf.
- His *Manhaj* of being against partisanship and hizbiyyah.
- His warning against all forms of *taqlīd* and blind following in opposition to the truth.
- His not judging truth based upon the majority, slogan and name of a sect but rather by its adherence to Islām.
- His *Manhaj* of not allowing the layperson to lend his ear or heart to people of *shirk*, *bidᶜah* and misguidance.
- His call not being limited to book of Allāh and Sunnah of the Messenger of Allāh (ﷺ) but also the way of the Ṣahābah [Salaf].
- His focus of daᶜwah being upon knowledge and admonishing the people to read the Qurʾān and books of Ḥadīth and the righteous scholars of this Ummah.
- His deep rooted knowledge of the various sects of the subcontinent and then emanating this knowledge to the masses so that they can stay away from there evil.
- His adherence to the Manhaj of listening to and obeying the muslim ruler (that is not to rebel against them) thus opposing the Khawārij.
- His respect for the Imāms of the religion whilst holding that they were not infallible and committed mistakes.

The second noble characteristic that I would like to briefly mention of the noble Shaikh is his sticking and referring to the Kibār (senior) Salafī scholars of this ummah. I say this because the Shaikh was a very humble person and teacher and had great wisdom in uniting the people upon truth.

The Shaikh revolutionised the monthly magazine's in Urdu and English medium from the 1980's onwards which would be dispatched throughout the entire world spreading the daᶜwah of the book and Sunnah. If one refers to these magazines then a person would be hard pressed to find any magazine published by the Shaikh which did not refer to the verdicts of the Kibār *ᶜUlamāʾ* of Saudi ᶜArabia such as

Shaikh Ibn Bāz, Shaikh al-ᶜUthaymīn and others of the *Lajnah al-Dā'imah* (counsel of senior scholars of Saudi ᶜArabia) as well as the senior scholars of the subcontinent and they are too many to cite here It was due to his love of the senior scholars that the Shaikh invited them to the United Kingdom. The Shaikh's love of the senior scholars of this Ummah played a pivotal role in nurturing thousands of youth and elders throughout Europe to love honour and respect the Scholars of Salafīyyah whilst at the same time introducing the daᶜwah of these scholars to the masses.

The short treatise you have before you is a precise yet detailed work of the Shaikh on the subject of *bidᶜah* so that to clarify to the masses the arguments and misguidance of the people of innovation. It is anticipated that there will be a detailed work on *bidᶜah* including a precise refutation of the principles of the people of *bidᶜah* and various misguided sects, In Shāʾ Allāh.

In this treatse the brothers have added detailed beneficial notes increasing the comprehension of the treatise, as well as further references. All of the Shaikhs words are in the made body of the text and all footnotes are by the researchers. They have also compiled the most comprehensive and detailed biography of the Shaikh and included it as part of this treatise.

May Allāh bless the Shaikh for all his noble efforts and the translators and researchers of the Shaikhs work. May Allāh put this in their balance of good deeds and may it be a means of salvation for them in the ākhirah. Amīn.

Abū Rumaisah Taimore Afẓal
Salafī Research Institute
Birmingham, England.
Jumada al-Ūla 1437H / March 2016

Shaikh Maḥmūd Aḥmad Mirpūrī

The Shaikhs Credentials

> B.A. Islamic studies, M.A ^{c}Arabic, Graduate of Dars Niẓāmī, Graduate of Madīnah University, Cheif Editor of Ṣirāt al-Mustaqīm, Managing Editor of The Straight Path, Secretary General of Jam^{c}ah Ahl al-Ḥadīth United Kingdom, General Secretary of Islamic Sharī^{c}ah Council of Britain, Convenor of Majlis Tahafuẓ Maqāmāt Muqaddisah, Khaṭīb at Green Lane Masjid and Director of Birmingham Muslim Community Centre.

He is the Shaikh, the ālim, the learned, Mahmūd Aḥmad Mirpūrī bin Nūr Muḥammad bin Muḥammad Ḥasan.

The Shaikh had a prolific personality and a phenomenal standing within the community so much so and to such an extent that no one has rivalled him even remotely in Britain with regards to his Dīn, his socio-political activism and his visionary academic writings. He was indeed from amongst the first people who propagated the true call of Tawḥīd in forsaken Europe. He rejuventated the Ahl al-Ḥadīth in the United Kingdom and paved a way to call to the truth. He expounded the call to the Qur$^{\circ}$ān and Sunnah without comprising the truth.

The Shaikh was born on the 6th of March 1945 corresponding to the 21st of Rab^{c}i ul-Awwal 1364H on a Tuesday. He was born in the area of Nagyāl, in Mirpūr district which is in present day Āzād Kashmīr. This general area is known as Panyām and has always been associated with the ideology of Ahl al-Ḥadīth for a long time. His Father was Shaikh Nūr Muḥammad who was very religious and learned. His grandfather was Hājī Muḥammed Ḥasan who was highly respected and known for his piety.

A few months after the Shaikhs birth his mother passed away and his maternal grandfather Muḥammad Ḥasan helped with his up bringing. After a few years the Shaikh's father also passed away and he was orphaned.

aned. The Shaikh was also an only child and thus had no siblings. The Shaikhs care resorted to his paternal uncle who started looking after him.

His Education

The Shaikh passed the 8th class at school in an area known as Chamāl which was local to him. The Shaikh had a very strong inclination for the Dīn from a very early age and would often recite the Qur'ān abundantly whilst at school. The Shaikhs father longed for him to study the sciences of the Dīn. When the Shaikh was a little older his family ie his uncle and grandfather aided his fathers wishes and encouraged his perusal of the sacred sciences. When the Shaikh passed his middle exams he was enrolled into the prestigious Institute and University of Gujranwāla known as Jāmia Islāmīyyah in Pākistān and this is where his Islamic education began.

At time the great scholar, al-Allāmah Muḥaddith Muḥammad Gondalwī and his student Shaikh Abu'l Barkāt Aḥmad were teaching at Jāmia Islāmīyyah Gujranwāla. So the Shaikh studied with these two great scholars and luminaries of their time as well as other scholars. The Shaikh was active and possessed great zeal and fervour for the Dīn and the *Manhaj* of Ahl al-Ḥadīth. He would participate in knowledge based discussions, scholastic debates and would often write academic articles for the various magazines and journals.

When Shaikh Maḥmūd Aḥmad was studying with these Shaikhs a number of well known scholar of the Ahl al-Ḥadīth were also studying at this prestigious institute. They included the likes of Shaikh Muḥammad Aʿẓam, Shaikh Ḥafīẓ ur-Rehmān Lakhawī, Allāmah Eḥsān Ilāhī Ẓahīr, Shaikh Thanāullāh Siālkotī and Shaikh Muḥammad Ḥayāt Dhaskawī and many others. From amongst the most well known was Shaikh Eḥsān Ilāhī Ẓahīr who was his senior, both Shaikhs got acquainted with each other and developed a close friendship and bond which continued until Shaikh Maḥmūds death. The closeness and strength of this friendship was further demonstrated with events that unfolded.

Shaikh Maḥmūd and Shaikh Thanāullāh Siālkotī also developed a close friendship which continued whilst both of them resided in England. Shaikh Thanāullāh also collated and compiled Shaikh Maḥmūd's articles and Fatāwa. The Shaikh was very independent and astute, as well as studying the Dīn he always thought one should not rely on the Dīn to earn a source of income and hence set up a little business and started to make some clothes with a powered loom. The Shaikh continued this until he relocated, this was his source of income which he was very content with. The Shaikh received and continued his early education whilst he was in Jāmia Islāmīyyah in Gujranwāla and passed his ᶜArabic scholar exams and his matriculation (equivalent to GCSE's), whilst he studied with the likes of Shaikh Muḥammad Gondalwī and others. After graduating from Jāmia Islāmīyyah Gujranwāla the Shaikh enrolled at the Islamic University of Bahāwalpūr in pursuit of knowledge. The Shaikh studied here for a few years with teachers of other methodologies. The Shaikh became the vice president of the student union during his time and in this regard he also received the first position and prize in a competition for the best speech. The Shaikh graduated from the University with Bachelor of Arts.

The Shaikh then enrolled in the ᶜArabic Oriental College, Punjāb University in Lahore, Pākistān and graduated with an M.A. (Master of Arts) in ᶜArabic with Honours with a first in 1971. After graduating the Shaikh worked as the editor of a weekly Ahl al-Ḥadīth newspaper called *'Ahle Ḥadīth'* in 1971, published in Lahore. At the same time time the Shaikh was also the Khaṭīb of the grand Ahl al-Ḥadīth Masjid in Begum Kot in Lahore. Another close friend and colleague of Shaikh Maḥmūd Aḥmad Mirpūrī and another teacher of ours, Shaikh Dr. Bahā al-Dīn Muḥammad Suleimān; the famous author and historian of the Ahl al-Ḥadīth, both studied together at the ᶜArabic Oriental College. When both Shaikhs came to England Shaikh Maḥmūd requested Dr. Bahā al-Dīn Muḥammad Suleimān to move to Birmingham from Edinburgh to aid and assist the daᶜwah.

Shaikh Maḥmūd then received a scholarship in late 1971 for the prestigious and illustrious Madīnah University, where he completed his further studies. Whilst at the University he studied with the great scholars of Madīnah and other than them who were living there at the time. The Shaikh then spent the following 5 years at the University and graduted in 1976 from the faculty of Sharīᶜah.

Whilst the Shaikh was in Madīnah he learnt and spent time with some of the great luminaries of this ummah as well as other great scholars in their own right. These include the likes of Shaikh Muḥammad Nāṣir al-Dīn al-Albānī, Shaikh ᶜAbdul ᶜAzīz ibn ᶜAbd Allāh ibn Bāz, Shaikh Muḥammad bin ᶜAbdul Wahhāb al-Banna, Shaikh Maḥfūz ar Rahman Zainallāh and many others.

After graduating he was sent to England from Saudi ᶜArabia. Now the Shaikh was in new territory which was alien to him. The Shaikh with his extensive knowledge, wisdom, intelligence and amazing interpersonal and communication skills spread the message of Tawḥīd, adhering to the Sunnah and the clear pristine Salafī *Manhaj*.

His Teachers

The Shaikh learnt directly from many great scholars who were well known for their knowledge and upholding the Sunnah. The speciality of the Shaikh also was that he called to pure daᶜwah Salafīyyah and pushed the *Manhaj* of Ahl al-Ḥadīth. What is further amazing about the Shaikh is that he also learnt from scholars who were from the deviant backgrounds whilst at Bahāwalpūr University yet he was firm and strong as they were teaching at the University and not by choice. From his numerous teachers were the likes of,

1. Shaikh al-Ḥadīth the Imām Ḥāfiẓ Muḥammed Gondalwī
2. Shaikh al-Ḥadīth Abuᵓl Barkāt Aḥmad
3. Shaikh Nazīr Aḥmad Khokar
4. Shaikh ᶜAbdul Gaffār Ḥasan
5. Shaikh Ḥammād al-Anṣārī
6. Shaikh Muḥammed Amān al-Jāmī
7. Shaikh ᶜAbdul Muḥsin al-ᶜAbbād
8. Shaikh Aḥmad Majzūb

The following teachers were not from an Ahl al-Ḥadīth background and the Shaikh studied with them whilst they were teaching at the Islamic University of Bahāwalpūr,

9. Shams al-Ḥaqq Afghānī
10. ᶜAbdur Rashīd Nuᶜmānī
11. Aḥmed Saᶜīd Kāzimī

He also benefited from the various teachers who were teaching in Madīnah University and Punjāb University whilst he was studying there.

He also benefited from the likes of Shaikh Badᶜi al-Dīn Sindhī, Shaikh Muḥammad Nāṣir al-Dīn al-Albānī, Shaikh ᶜAbdul ᶜAzīz ibn ᶜAbd Allāh ibn Bāz, Shaikh ᶜAbdul Muḥsin al-ᶜAbbād, Shaikh ᶜAbdul Ghaffār Ḥasan Rehmānī, Shaikh Muḥammad bin ᶜAbdul Wahhāb al-Banna, Shaikh Eḥsān Ilāhī Zahīr and many others.

His Travels

The Shaikh travelled to numerous countries calling people to Allāh and raised the call of Ahl al-Ḥadīth ie the Qurᵓān and Sunnah. Some of these travels were to Islamic conferences as well as research seminars.

He travelled to Saudi ᶜArabia, Egypt, Syria, Indonesia, U.A.E., Holland, Germany, Belgium, Denmark and Pākistān and participated in numerous Islamic symposiums where he expounded the call of the Qurᵓān and Sunnah. In 1982 he attended a seminar in Pākistān on Qaḍa ie being a Qaḍī, issuing rulings and Fatāwa. He informed the scholars of his activities and daᶜwah efforts. Everyone was happy and pleased with him, his efforts and his accomplishments in the west.

Early History of the Daᶜwah in England

Prior to Shaikh Maḥmūds arrival in England, Shaikh Faḍal Karīm Āᶜṣim and Mawlana ᶜAbdul Karīm Thāqib had already set up Markazī Jamāᶜah Ahl al-Ḥadīth and had a few branches elsewhere under which the organisation was fulfilling its duty of daᶜwah. There was however no formal structure or any specific organisation.

Shaikh Faḍal Karīm Āᶜṣim with the aide of some associates started to use a house in Alum Rock, Birmingham for their activities and also established a madrassah in 1975. It so happened that in the same year in the summer of 1975 a Saudi delegation on the order of Dār al-Daᶜwah wa'l-Irshād wa'l Iftā, whose president was Shaikh ᶜAbdul ᶜAziz ibn ᶜAbd Allāh ibn Bāz, was sent to the United Kingdom for research and daᶜwah.

The head of this delegation was the great Shaikh Muḥammad ᶜAbdul Wahhāb al-Banna and he was accompanied by the well known Albanian Ḥadīth Master, Shaikh Muḥammad Nāṣir al-Dīn al-Albānī. They were also accompanied by translators who were students of knowledge in their own right and studying in Madīnah University at the time. They were asked to accompany the delegation because of the large exodus of the Asian community from the subcontinent.

The delegation was accompanied by Shaikh Maḥmūd Aḥmad Mirpūrī, Shaikh Major Muḥammad Aslam and Sharīf Aḥmad Ḥāfiẓ. Shaikh Faẓal Karīm Āᶜṣim tirelessly helped them whilst they engaged in daᶜwah and propagated the call of Tawḥīd. The delegation was highly impressed and pleased with Shaikh Faẓal Karīm Āᶜṣim's efforts and diligence and acknowledged the speed and rate of his work.

They also noticed the need for further callers to help Shaikh Faẓal Karīm Āᶜṣim and he also expressed the need for young active yet knowledgable callers to come to the United Kingdom and assist with daᶜwah to the rapidly growing Muslim community in their thousands. The delegation advised him to go and meet Shaikh ᶜAbdul ᶜAzīz ibn ᶜAbd Allāh ibn Bāz and request further assistance as he was the Head of Dār al-Iftā.

During December of the same year ie 1975 Shaikh Faḍal Karīm Āᶜṣim went for Ḥajj and also met Shaikh Ibn Bāz and he mentioned his request for help. He explained the need for daᶜwah and the growing Muslim population and how western society was influencing them and how the Muslims were contravening a dejected path.

Shaikh Ibn Bāz asked Shaikh Faḍal Karīm Āᶜṣim how he could help him. Shaikh Faḍal Karīm Āᶜṣim said the three students that came with the Islamic University delegation during the summer could they be sent to the United Kingdom to him. Shaikh Ibn Bāz was very pleased with the request and sent Shaikh Maḥmūd Aḥmad Mirpūrī and

Sharīf Aḥmad Ḥāfiẓ to United Kingdom for Daᶜwah and teaching at the behest of al-Daᶜwah waᵓl Irshād waᵓl Iftā during the latter part of 1976 when they both had completed their studies.

At the time Shaikh ᶜAbdul Karīm Thāqib was already in England and graduated from the Islamic University of Madīnah and and had already started working with Shaikh Faḍal Karīm Āᶜṣim. After coming to England the Shaikh further expounded the call of Ahl al-Ḥadīth with the aid and help of some close friends and people on the Qurᵓān and Sunnah. They started the work of daᶜwah in Birmingham in Alum Rock and then moved to Green Lane Masjid. Slowly but surely the daᶜwah efforts which started in Birmingham spread to other cities and a number of masjids started being built.

At the very onset Shaikh Maḥmūd Aḥmad Mirpūrī formed an organised structure with relevant departments. He gathered all the people upon the methodology of Ahl al-Ḥadīth and presented his vision and direction for the Ahl al-Ḥadīth There is no doubt the Shaikh was a visionary and an illuminary with an aim and goal for future generations.

Shaikh Maḥmūd then travelled up and down the country and his life had become in establishing an organisation based on the Qurᵓān and Sunnah and he spent a lot of his time on it. He visited many different cities and towns giving the people daᶜwah and informing them of the great benefits and rewards in calling to Allāh and spreading the message of Tawḥīd.

With the Shaikhs hard work branches were set up in all major cities and then teaching institutes followed where thousands of students would gain knowledge of the Dīn. This trend became stronger and the organisations strength grew and it became well established and solid in it's core belief and ideology so much so that it was the only organisation to grow so quick and strong and an example compared to any other organisation in the whole of Europe.

Shaikh Maḥmūd Aḥmad Mirpūrī was also instrumental and played a central role in forming and establishing the 'Islamic Sharīᶜah Council' which was set up to deal with the domestic issues of the Muslims whilst living in the United Kingdom. These issues ranged from marriage, divorce, *Khula* etc.

Islamic Conferences

The Shaikh would instigate the organisation of conferences and seminars throughout the United Kingdom. He would also organise regular conferences wherein the Shaikh would call renowned scholars, dignitaries and other people of standing.

We have already mentioned the Shaikh had great respect for the senior scholars and thus in this regard he invited the likes of Shaikh Badᶜi al-Dīn Sindhī, Shaikh Eḥsān Ilāhi Ẓahīr, Shaikh Muḥammad ibn ᶜAbd Allāh al-Subayyal, Shaikh ᶜAzīz Zubaidī, Shaikh Sāleḥ Ibn al-Ḥumaid, Shaikh Ṣafī al-Rahman al-Mubārakpūrī, Shaikh Ṣalāh al-Dīn Yūsuf, Shaikh Irshād al-Ḥaq al-Atharī, Shaikh ᶜAbdul Wakīl Ḥashmī, Shaikh Muḥammad Ḥussain Shaikhupūrī, Qāri ᶜAbdul Ḥafīẓ, Shaikh Faẓal Ḥaq and others.

Ṣirāṭ al-Mustaqīm and The Straight Path

Prior to Shaikh Maḥmūd coming to England, Shaikh Faḍal Karīm Āᶜṣim and Shaikh ᶜAbdul Karīm Thāqib had already set up and started the Ṣirāṭ al-Mustaqīm magazine. They would painstakingly write it out by hand and then have it printed. Shaikh Maḥmūd transformed the magazine; he changed the language style, the range of articles, its design, layout and printing quality. Ṣirāṭ al-Mustaqīm is still in production to this day.

The Shaikh felt the need to work on the English speaking community and thus began publishing an English monthly magazine called 'The Straight Path.' This magazine became very popular and very effective during its time.

His Writings

The Shaikh was a prolific writer and over the years he penned hundred of writings. The Shaikh would write in every issue of the Ṣirāṭ al-Mustaqīm journal on monthly basis. In the early days the magazine went through changes where it would be published weekly and fortnightly. The Shaikh would answer questions in the magazine and he also had a regular column where he would share his thought on current issues which were direct and to the point. The Shaikh was also the editor in chief and would thus write beneficial and thought provoking editorials which are also considered to be part of his writing skills and journalism.

The Shaikh would also write scholastic articles in various magazines, when he was in Pākistān and in Saudi ᶜArabia. Most of his writings in the Ṣirāṭ al-Mustaqīm have been collated and published by his close companion and friend Shaikh Thanāullāh and they are as follows

1.Maqālāt Maḥmūd

This was first published 8 years after the Shaikhs death in 1996 and consists of four treatise's over 200 pages.

(a) Every Innovation is Misguidance
(b) The Fitnah of the Rejectors of Ḥadīth
(c) The Emergence of the Maḥdī
(d) The Unlawfulness of Interest.

2. Fatāwa Ṣirāṭ al-Mustaqīm.

This was first published in approximately 1996 and consists of Fatāwa on a wide range of issues spanning 570 pages. It was reprinted in 1999 and in 2001. It has also been selectively rendered into English by Shaikh ᶜAbdul Hādī al-ᶜUmarī In 1998

2. Talkh Wa Shīrī (The Bitter and Sweet)

These were the Shaikhs commentaries, notes and opinions on a wide range of issues from socio-political, daily life, events etc. The Shaikh started writing this in his monthly column in the Ṣirāṭ al-Mustaqīm magazine from 1986. This was also published 8 years afrer his death in 1996 and it spans 439 pages.

The Shaikh in the later years of his life also wanted to write a Tafsīr of the Qurʾān. The Shaikh had numerous other articles as mentioned in the various magazines from the days when he was a student in Jāmia Islāmīyyah Gujranwāla as well as when he was the editor of the weekly Ahle Ḥadīth newspaper. Shaikh also had a fervour to publish and distribute books. In this regard he aided the publication of numerous books the most notable of was a book on the legal status of the Sunnah of Shaikh ᶜAbdul Ghaffār Ḥasan Rehmānī.

His Etiquettes and Manners

He was extremely pleasant in his nature. He would always be well dressed and would be softly spoken with a gentle voice. He would always speak kindly and nicely to people and whoever he would speak to would he highly influenced by his kind nature and personality. His face would often reflect his outstanding level of intelligence and intellect. He was extremely articulate and precise in his speech in how he addressed people and crowds. He was one of the most effective propagators and callers to Islām in the west in the last 25 years.

The Shaikh very much adopted the teachings of the Qurʾān and Ḥadīth and would try his utmost best to reconcile between differing parties. There are numerous examples of this but the most notable is when the Shaikh invited Shaikh Eḥsān Ilāhi Ẓahīr and Shaikh Faẓal Ḥaq to the United Kingdom with sole intent of bringing about reconciliation between them after a disagreement arose between them regarding the Jamāᶜah. This was successful but then eventually fizzled out due to a perioid of inactivity.

Shaikh Maḥmūd Aḥmad Mirpūrī had great love and reverence for the people of Ḥadīth and likewise and similarly he would be very upset and saddened by the various unnecessary differences amongst the Ahl al-Ḥadīth so much so that on one occasion he travelled to Pākistān to facilitate a reconciliation between two opposing parties. This shows how much concern and adoration he had for his fellow Salafīs. The Shaikh was always inclined to bring about good and praiseworthy outcomes in any situation which was a refection of his concern for the people of the Sunnah and the Ahl al-Ḥadīth.

The Shaikh had great *taqwa* and great humility which was universally known about him. He was humble, down to earth, friendly and approcable. He despised praise and all unwarranted acclaim. There are numerous examples of this, we recall that once we spoke to the great historian of the Salafīs and Ahl al-Ḥadīth, Shaikh Ṣalāḥ al-

Dīn Yūsuf who narrated to us that Shaikh Maḥmūd Aḥmad Mirpūrī once said to him that if you ever need to mention me then do so without any great detail or honoury titles. This was indeed from the humility and humbleness of our Shaikh, *Rahimahullāh.*

The Shaikh was also very active and instrumental in some of the socio-political issues of his era. He was at the forefront during the Rushdi affair and vehemently opposed the imprudent and slanderous accusation against Saudi ᶜArabia. He would highlight and regularly talk about the issue of Palestine and even more so he was actively involved in the Kashmīr liberation movement.

What the Scholars said about him when he died

Shaikh Badᶜi al-Dīn Shāh al-Rāshidī al-Sindhī wrote, *"I was very shocked after hearing the news of the tragic death of Faḍīlat ul-Shaykh Mawlāna Maḥmūd Aḥmad Mirpūrī. May Allāh accept his efforts and service with regards to propagating and spreading Islām in the foreign lands, May Allāh forgive his mistakes, raise his status and grant the whole Jamāᶜah strength to cope with this tragedy. Amīn, as the whole Jamāᶜah is equally grieving and may Allāh allow us to die upon Islām."*

Shaikh ᶜAbdul ᶜAzīz ibn ᶜAbd Allāh Bāz said, *"The news of the tragic death of Maḥmūd Aḥmad Mirpūrī reached me. May Allāh forgive the Shaikhs shortcomings and grant him mercy and may he grant you wholesome patience. May Allāh give the Shaikhs children guidance and success to tread upon his path and grant us an equal replacement, Amīn. We all belong to Allāh to him we shall return."* (ᶜAbdul ᶜAzīz bin ᶜAbd Allāh bin Bāz - Dār al-Iftā, Riyāḍh)

Shaikh ᶜAbdul Qādir Ḥabībullāh al-Sindhī wrote: *"Me, my father and my household are all grieving with you. Kindly convey my condolences to the Jamāᶜah, the Shaikhs family and children, as I am also a member of this Jamāᶜah. I praise the efforts of Jamāᶜah Ahl al-Ḥadīth United Kingdom. I was impressed with the Shaikh's praiseworthy and noble efforts and I ask Allāh to accept this from him and to replace him with someone beneficial for the Jamāᶜah Ahl al-Ḥadīth. May Allāh also grant success in further propapagting the Dīn and its teachings and may he give you and all of us patience. Amīn."* (Shaikh ᶜAbdul Qādir Ḥabībullāh al-Sindhī - Professor Islamic University Madīnah)

Shaikh Ṣafī al-Rahman al-Mubārakpūrī wrote, *"The Shaikh had raised the knowledge of Islām in the land of kufr and upheld the burden of rectification in this land of anarchy. Due to his effort, struggle, understanding, contemplations, wisdom and intelligence he raised the rank of the Ahl al-Ḥadīth of Britain from being virtually unknown and non-existant to the epitomy and vast stature of society. Without doubt everyone played a role in this formation and Inshaᵓ Allāh everyone will be rewarded accordingly for their efforts. Thus the pivotal role the Shaikh played is not in need of any clarification. We have hope in our Rabb the most generous and oft giving and we supplicate to him that he grants the Shaikh the loftiest of stations and that he is blessed, favoured, forgiven and compassion. My heart pains after contantly thinking that a very capable and an adept visionary leader passed away. Death is undoubtedly a stark reality and its time and place is also definitive and so when a tragic event like this occurs the heart is affected and old thoughts become active. I pray to Allāh that he grants the Shaikh his special blessings and that he grants his close relatives virtuous patience and that he replaces the Shaikh with someone beneficial for all of us."* (Shaikh Ṣafī al-Rahman al-Mubārakpūrī - Markaz Khidmah al-Sunnah Waᵓl Sīrah al-Nabawīyyah - Islamic University Madīnah)

Shaikh Dr. ᶜAbd Allāh bin ᶜAbdul Muḥsin al-Turkī said, *"I have receieved news in great sorrow of the tragic death of Shaikh Maḥmūd Aḥmad Mirpūrī, his son Faiṣal and his mother in law who returned to Allāh and also the news that some of the family members were injured. I would like to offer my deep condolences to the family on the deaths of the family members. I am aware and well acquainted with Shaikh Maḥmūd Aḥmad efforts in repelling atheism and propagating the true Islamic teachings and I salute him for his outstanding efforts.*

(Summarised)" (Dr. ᶜAbd Allāh ibn ᶜAbdul Muḥsin al-Turkī - Director Imām Muḥammad bin Saᶜud University)

Shaikh Muḥammad ibn ᶜAbd Allāh al-Subayyal said, *"I heard of the grief stricken death of the Secretary General of the Jamāᶜah Ahl al-Ḥadīth Shaikh Maḥmūd Aḥmad Mirpūrī with great sadness and sorrow. We all belong to Allāh and to Him we shall return. May Allāh give him a lofty place in His infinite Paradise and he give you and the Shaikh's family patience. Amīn."* (Shaikh Muḥammad bin ᶜAbd Allāh al-Subayyal - Imām and Khaṭīb of Haram Makkah.)

Shaikh ᶜAzīz Zubaidī said, *"I read today in the newspaper that my beloved friend and the Secretary general of Jamāᶜah Ahl al-Ḥadīth Britain, Shaikh Maḥmūd Aḥmad Mirpūrī passed away, To Allāh we below and to him we will return. Shaikh Mirpūrī was returning from a Daᶜwah programme and such journeys had become the norm in his life. This news shocked me and what is more upsetting is that I do not know who to offer my condolences to... (summarized)"*

Shaikh Muḥammad ibn Qaᶜud and Shaikh ᶜAlī ibn Fahd ibn Gaith said, *"We received news with extreme sadness of the tragic death of Shaikh Maḥmūd Aḥmad Mirpūrī in a car accident. May Allāh shade the Shaikh in His Mercy and Pardon, may He forgive him, you and us and give us an equally good representative. We hope that you will convey our emotions to the family and his colleagues. We all belong to Allāh and to Him we will return."* (Shaikh Muḥammad bin Ibrāhīm bin Qaᶜud, Shaikh Fahd bin Gaith - Dār al-Iftā, Riyaḍh)

Numerous other great scholars of Ahl al-Ḥadīth and other than them offered their condolences. As the Shaikh was very active and had a dynamic personality he thus had a phenomenol amount of interaction between a wide range of people. Some of the learned people and dignatories who offered their condolences include the likes of Shaikh ᶜAbdul Ḥamīd Reḥmāni – Abuᶜl Kalām Islamic Centre India, Shaikh ᶜAbdur Rahman Salafī – Amīr Jamāᶜah Ghurabā Ahl al-Ḥadīth, Shaikh ᶜAbdur Salām Reḥmanī – Sec. Gen. Jamāᶜah Ahl al-Ḥadīth India, Shaikh Maḥmūd Murād – Quran & Sunnah Society Canada,

Shaikh Mian Faḍal Ḥaq – Gen. Sec Jamāᶜah Ahl al-Ḥadīth Pākistān, Shaikh ᶜAbdur Rashīd Butt – Jamāᶜah Ahl al-Ḥadīth Jammu Kashmīr, Shaikh ᶜAbdul Mālik Mujāḥid – Dar us-Salām Books, Shaikh Bashīr Anṣārī – Editor al-Islām, Shaikh ᶜAbd Allāh Gurdāspūrī – Jamāᶜah Ahl al-Ḥadīth Pākistān, Shaikh Muḥammad Ḥussain Shaikhupūrī – The orator of Pākistān, Shaikh Ṣalaḥ al-Dīn Yūsuf – Famous author from Pākistān, Prince Bandār bin Sulṭān bin ᶜAbdul ᶜAzīz- Saudi Ambassador to US, Prince Muḥammad bin Faiṣal bin Turkī – Director of religious affairs and many others.

The Shaikhs Family

The Shaikh had three sons, Faiṣal Maḥmūd, Abdul Awwal Maḥmūd and Aqeel Maḥmūd.

Faiṣal Maḥmūd was born in 1981. The two compilers of this biography were in the same class as Faiṣal. Even at a young age Faiṣal had exemplary manners and ettiquetes. He was astute, vibrant and very kind. He would always share sweets with us in class. He is dearly missed by all those who knew him pray that Allāh grants him a place in Jannah. Amīn

ᶜAbdul Awwal, the eldest was born in 1978. He has always been active in daᶜwah and religious affairs. He studied in Jāmia Islāmīyyah Madīnah for a while from 1999 until 2002, he had to terminate his studies due to unforeseen circumstances. He also managed the English journal, 'The Straight Path' for a short while from 2005 until 2007. He has migrated from the United Kingdom and is still active in daᶜwah.

Aqeel was born in 1984. He is very active in daᶜwah and conducts regular lessons and seminars throughout the United Kingdom. He graduated from Jāmia Islāmīyyah Madīnah from the faculty of Shariᶜah in 2011, the same faculty as his father, the Shaikh. He is also a Ḥāfiẓ of the Qur᾿ān and currently lives with his family in Birmingham.

The Shaikhs Death

The Shaikh was travelling from Newcastle to Birmingham in the early hours of the morning with his family. The Shaikhs car had broken down in the middle lane of the M6 motorway in Cheshire and a large vehicle ploughed into them. The Shaikh, his eldest son, Faiṣal and his mother in law died instantly in the accident. The Shaikhs wife and son, Aqeel sustained serious injuries and were taken to hospital.

We still remember the day vividly when our Shaikh *Rahimahullāh* died on 10th October 1988. when the Shaikh was only 43 years old.

This is a very brief biography of our teacher, Shaikh Maḥmūd Aḥmad Mirpūrī and it by no means serves justice to the life, works and efforts of this visionary reformer of the Salafi's and Ahl al-Ḥadīth in the United Kingdom. He Rahimahullāh left behind a great legacy and hundreds of students who continue his legacy. We make Du[c]ā and supplicate to Allāh Jalo Wa A[c]la that he grants our Shaikh, his family and all the Muslims a place in Jannah. Amīn

By the two students of the Shaikh
who are in dire need of your Du[c]ā's

Abū Ḥibbān Malak
Abū Khuzaimah [c]Imrān Masoom Anṣārī
30th Jumada al-Ūla 1437H / Thursday 10th March 2016
Birmingham, England.

Important Principles

Allāh The Most High said,

لَقَدْ كَانَ لَكُمْ فِي رَسُولِ ٱللَّهِ أُسْوَةٌ حَسَنَةٌ لِّمَن كَانَ يَرْجُوا۟ ٱللَّهَ وَٱلْيَوْمَ ٱلْءَاخِرَ وَذَكَرَ ٱللَّهَ كَثِيرًا ﴿٢١﴾

> **There has certainly been for you in the Messenger of Allāh an excellent pattern for anyone whose hope is in Allāh and the Last Day and [who] remembers Allāh often.** (Sūrah al-Aḥzab:21)

In light of this blessed āyah[1] we can say only the Messenger of Allāh (ﷺ) is worthy to be followed and obeyed in all the issues and affairs of the Dīn. Therefore, whatever the Messenger of Allāh (ﷺ) instructed us or taught us, is only worthy to be followed and no one has the right or capacity to add or to remove anything from it.[2] Just as Allāh is alone

[1] This is a tremendous āyah of the Qurʾān and in it are many benefits. ʿAbdur Rahmān Nāṣir as-Saʿdī states in his explanation of this āyah in his book *'Taysīr ul-Karīm ur-Rahman Fī Tafsīr Kalām ul-Manān'* that, *'The people of Uṣūl [principles and jurisprudence] have mentioned that this āyah is an evidence to show that the actions [afāl] of the Messenger of Allāh (ﷺ) are an evidence to be followed in the Dīn. The principal is that 'The actions of the Messenger of Allāh (ﷺ) are an evidence in the legislation of Islām for all to follow until such time that a further evidence exists to restrict his actions as being specific only for him'. It should be known that the uswah [example] is generally of two types Ḥasanah [pure] and Sayyiʿa [evil]. So the prophets example is always pure. Indeed, when the prophets asked the people to follow their pure example the people replied 'but the luxurious ones among them said:* ***"We found our fathers following a certain way and religion, and we will indeed follow their footsteps." [az-Zukhruf:22].*** *So it can be seen that they chose an example to follow which was evil over that which is pure and it is only through the guidance and mercy of Allāh that one can be guided to the pure example of the prophets to follow."* Allāh's aid is sought.

[2] Some ignorant people who advocate strict blind following of modern day madhabs say, that we are always pushing people to learn the book and Sunnah and yet there was no Bukhārī, Muslim, Abū Dāwūd etc at the time of the Messenger of Allāh (ﷺ) and his companions so is this not itself a *bidʿah*? Then to these ones there is no point

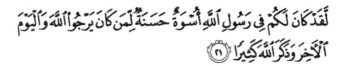

without a partner, nothing should be associated with him in terms of his essence and attributes because this is clear *shirk* even if they are a prophet or a holy saint.[3]

Likewise and similarly, the guidance the Messenger of Allāh (ﷺ) gave us about the Dīn, it is impermissible to change it in any way. We cannot add anything to it from ourselves and then continue to call it our Dīn. Thereby thinking that we will achieve reward, this is indeed innovation.[4] The path that opposes the way of the Sunnah[5] of the Messenger of Allāh (ﷺ) and the companions is unacceptable in the Dīn. This is because the Messenger of Allāh (ﷺ) said,

giving any long winded answer except to say that at the noble era of the Messenger of Allāh (ﷺ) tribes of the Muhājirūn would visit the Anṣār of Madīnah to be educated in the religion. One such tribe was that of ᶜAbdul Qays who said *"The Anṣār would teach us the book of our Lord and the Sunnah of our Prophet."* [Aḥmad Ibn Ḥanbal, *al-Musnad* [no.15131] Allāh's aid is sought from such ignorance.

[3] Cf. what is the reality of *shirk* and its different forms [Maḥmūd Aḥmad Mirpūrī, *Fatāwa Ṣirāt al-Mustaqīm* [pp.33-38].

[4] The Albanian Ḥadīth Master, Muḥammad Nāṣir al-Dīn al-Albānī said, *"It is obligatory to have knowledge of innovations which have been introduced into the Dīn, recognizing them is very important because a believer can only get closer to Allāh by abstaining from innovations and this is only possible by knowing their reality. When a person does not know the principles and rules of innovations he will fall into them. This falls under the principle, 'that which does not allow an obligation to be fulfilled is also thus obligatory' as the scholars of Uṣūl have mentioned. Likewise, and similarly this also applies to shirk because whoever does not fully understand it will fall into it and this can be seen amongs the Muslims who intend to seek closeness to Allāh through polytheistic (shirk) actions. Like for example vowing to the Awliya and righteous, swearing by there names, circulating their graves and erecting mosques over themand other such actions which are known to be shirk according to the scholars. Thus, it is important to know the Sunnah pertaining to Ibādah and likewise it is also important to know its opposite ie innovations."* [al-Albānī, *al-Ajwabah al-Nāfiᶜah ᶜĀn Asilah Lajnah Masjid al-Jāmiᶜah* [pp.109-110]

[5] Ibn Rajab said, *"The Sunnah is the path that is traversed, thus it includes the adhering and holding onto the manhaj which the* Messenger of Allāh (ﷺ) *and his rightly guided Khulafā were upon, whether it is beliefs, actions or statements. This is the complete Sunnah."* [Ibn Rajab, *Jāmᶜe al-ᶜUlūm al-Ḥikam* [1:120]. Ahl al-Sunnah are known as this group because they attribute themselves to the Sunnah of the Messenger of Allāh (ﷺ) and accept his statements, actions and believe in him inwardly and outwardly. [cf. al-Fawzān, *Sharḥ ᶜAqīdah al-Wāsiṭiyyah* [p.10], al-ᶜUthaymīn, *Fatḥ al-Rabb al-Bariyyah Talkhīs al-Ḥamawiyyah* [p.10]

> "Hold firmly onto my Sunnah and the Sunnah of my righty guided Khulafā."[6]

Innovations are very dangerous actions and there are clear warnings from the Messenger of Allāh (ﷺ) concerning the serious consequences regarding an innovator. Hence, before we proceed into defining what innovations are ie *bid^{c}ah* and answer the doubts and confusion of the people of innovation and some of the common prevalent innovations, we would like to mention some of the statements of the Messenger of Allāh (ﷺ) in reprimand of innovations and innovators.[7] There occurs a Ḥadīth in *Ṣaḥīḥ Muslim* which states,

[6] *Tirmidhī* [no's 266, 2678], who graded it Ḥasan Ṣaḥīḥ. *Abū Dawūd* [no.4607], *Ibn Mājah* [no.42], *Dārimī* [no.296], *Ḥākim* [1:96]. It was also authenticated by al-Dhahabī and al-Albānī in his checking of Abū Dawūd. Narrated by ^{c}Irbād ibn Sāriyah as-Sulamī (رضي الله عنه). From amongst the known people of Suffa and lived in Homs, Shām. The Ḥadīth is also narrated from him by Jubair bin Nufayr, Abū Ruhm as-Sum^{c}ī, ^{c}Abdur Rahmān bin ^{c}Umara as-Sulamī. Aḥmad Ibn Ḥanbal said that ^{c}Irbād's kunya was Abū Najīh. He died in the year 75H. [al-Dhahabī, *Siyar ^{c}Alām an-Nabulā* of [3:419, 422]. On the authority of Abū Najīh al-^{c}Irbād ibn Sāriyah (رضي الله عنه) who said: *The Messenger of Allāh (ﷺ) gave us a sermon by which our hearts were filled with fear and tears came to our eyes. So we said, "O Messenger of Allāh! It is as though this is a farewell sermon, so counsel us." He (The Messenger of Allāh (ﷺ) said, "I counsel you to have taqwa (fear) of Allāh, and to listen and obey [your leader], even if a slave were to become your amīr. Verily he among you who lives long will see great controversy, so you must keep to my Sunnah and to the Sunnah of the Khulafā ar-Rāshidīn (the rightly guided caliphs), those who guide to the right way. Cling to it stubbornly [literally: with your molar teeth]. Beware of newly invented matters [in the religion], for verily every bid^{c}ah (innovation) is misguidance."*

[7] The following Ḥadīth highlights the severity of innovations, moreso in the sanctuaries, Ā^{c}ṣim narrates that he said to Anas (رضي الله عنه), *"Did Allāh's Messenger* Messenger of Allāh (ﷺ) *make Madīnah a sanctuary?" He replied, "Yes, (Madīnah is a sanctuary from such-and-such place to such-and-such place. It is forbidden to cut its trees, and whoever innovates an heresy in it or commits a sin therein, will incur the curse of Allāh, the Angels, and all the people." Then Mūsa bin Anas told me that Anas added, "..... or gives refuge to such a heretic or a sinner..."* [*Bukhārī* [no.7306], *Muslim* [no.1366]. al-Shāṭibī in explanation of this Ḥadīth said, *"From the generality of this Ḥadīth it includes everything that opposes the Sharī^{c}ah and the innovations are the most wicked."* [Shāṭibī, *al-Ei^{c}tisām* [1:69].

> "Verily the best of speech is the Book of Allāh and the best guidance is the guidance of Messenger of Allāh (ﷺ) and from the worst of the affairs are the novelties and every innovation is misguidance."[8]

The Messenger of Allāh (ﷺ) would often repeat these words during his sermons. There occurs another Ḥadīth in *Bukhārī*[9] and *Muslim*, its words are,

> "Whoever introduced something new in our affair, which was not from it, will have it rejected."[10]

The third Ḥadīth is also from *Bukhārī* in which Sahl ibn Saᶜd (رضي الله عنه)[11] narrates,

[8] *Muslim* [no.867], *Musnad Aḥmad* [14:126], *Abū Dawūd* [no.4608], *Tirmidhī* [no.2676] and *Mishkāt* [no.16]. Narrated by Jābir Ibn ᶜAbd Allāh (رضي الله عنه). He was the illustrious companion who partook in the pledge of al-Riḍhwān and from the early acceptors of Islām. A great scholar of the faith. The status and knowledge of his father is well known and documented. Cf. *Shudhrāt al-Dhahab* [1:319].

[9] Narrated by the Mother of the Believers, Āᶜishah (رضي الله عنها), daughter of Abū Bakr (رضي الله عنه) and the beloved wife of Prophet Muḥammad (ﷺ). In the fifty years following his death, she became a great teacher of Islām and preserved and transmitted over two thousand Aḥadīth. The Messenger of Allāh (ﷺ) married her in Shawwāl, a year after marrying Sawdah (رضي الله عنها). Āᶜishah (رضي الله عنها) was regarded as the best loved of all the Prophet's wives. She came under the loving care and attention of the Prophet Muḥammad (ﷺ) himself. As his wife and close companion, she acquired from him much knowledge and insight such as no woman has acquired. She was the most learned female Muslim jurist in history. She passed away in Ramaḍhān 17th, 57H, and was buried in Baqᶜī. There are 741 narrations from her in *Bukhārī* and 503 in *Muslim*. [*al-Isābah* [4:348 8:16-21], *Thiqāt* [3:323], *Tabaqāt* [8:39], *Sīyar Aᶜlam an-Nabulā* [2:135-201], *Tahdhīb al-Tahdhīb* [12:384 no.8989], *Taqrīb al-Tahdhīb* [no.8679]. *ᶜAsad al-Ghābah* [7:188], *al-Istiᶜāb* [4:1881], *Aᶜlām an-Nisā* [3:9], *al-Kāshif* [3:476], *Tahdhīb al-Kamāl* [3:1689], *Khulaṣah* [3:387], *al-Ḥilyah* [2:43], *Shadhrāt al-Dhahab* [1:61], *Tārīkh al-Saghīr* [1:99-103] and others.

[10] *Bukhārī* [no.2697], *Muslim* [no.1718], *Musnad Aḥmad* [6:146]. Āᶜẓimabādī, *Sunan Dārquṭnī Maᶜa Taᶜlīq al-Mughnī* [4:224-227], Ubaidullāh Mubārakpūrī, *Mishkāt al-Maṣābīḥ Maᶜa Mirᶜāh al-Mafātīḥ* [1:236 no.1400].

[11] The illustrious companion he is Sahl ibn Saᶜd bin Mālik bin Khālid bin Thaᶜlaba bin Hāritha bin ᶜAmr bin al-Khazraj (رضي الله عنه), born in Madīnah and was a great companion from amongst the Anṣār. He is the narrator of many ahādīth including 116 in Ṣaḥīḥ Bukhārī and 46 in Ṣaḥiḥ Muslim. From amongst those who he learnt and narrated from are: Prophet Muḥammad (ﷺ), ᶜUbayy ibn Kaᶜb, Āᶜṣim bin ᶜAdīy bin al-Jaᶜdd,

> I heard the The Messenger of Allāh (ﷺ) saying, "I am your predecessor at the Lake-Fount *(Kawthar)*, and whoever will come to it, will drink from it, and whoever will drink from it, will never become thirsty after that. There will come to me some people whom I know and they know me, and then a barrier will be set up between me and them."[12]

The fourth Ḥadīth is from Baihaqī,

> "Whoever honoured an innovator then he has collaborated in demolishing Islām" (*Shuᶜbal Imān* of Baihaqī)[13]

There are numerous other statements from the companions, the Imāms[14] and the *Awliyā* of this Ummah, which order us to abstain from innovations and to stay away from innovators. We present two such statements for the sake of brevity. Fuḍail ibn ᶜAyyāḍ, who has a high status with the Sūfīyyah,[15] he said,

ᶜAmr bin Aᶜbsa al-Salmī, Marwān bin al-Ḥakam bin Abī al-Āᶜs. He lived for around 100 years and was from amongst the last few companions to pass away in Madīnah. He died in 88 or 91H. [Cf. *al-Iṣābah* [3:200], *ath-Thiqāt* [3:168 no.550], *Tārīkh al-Kabīr* [4:97 no.2092], *Tahdhīb al-Tahdhīb* [4:229 no.2751] and *Taqrīb al-Tahdhīb* [no.2666], *al-Kāshif* [no.2192], *al-Jarḥ* [4:198 no.853] and al-*Kamāl* [12:188 no.2612]

[12] *Bukhārī* [no.7050]. Similar worded ḥadīth are narrated in Bukhārī by the companions Asmā, ᶜAbd Allāh, Abū Hurairah, Ibn al-Musayyīb and others.

[13] A similar wording statement is reported from one of the Salaf, Ibrāhīm bin Maīsarah which will be cited later.

[14] Abū Ḥanīfah said, *"Stick to the narrations and the way of the Salaf, and beware of newly-invented matters for all of it is innovation."* [Suyūṭī, *Sawn al-Mantaq* [p.32]. al-Bukhāri said, *"I have met more than a thousand scholars ... (then he named the more prominent in each of the lands he visited) and I found that they all agreed on the following points: ... they all used to prohibit bidᶜah - that which the Prophet and his Companions were not upon, because of the saying of Allāh, '...and hold fast to the rope of Allāh and do not separate."* [From his article on belief, quoted in *Sharḥ Uṣūl Eiᶜtiqād,* [1:170.] Amongst the scholars he met were Aḥmad bin Ḥanbal, Abū ᶜUbayd al-Qāsim, Ibn Maᶜīn, ibn Abī Āᶜṣim, Ibn Abī Shaybah, and Abū Ṣāleh the scribe of Laith bin Ṣaᶜd.

[15] There are numerous statements of the Sūfīyyah in reprimand and censure of *bidᶜah* and mentioning them here will lengthen the notes unnecessarily. Cf. Aḥmad al-Rūmi's

> "Whoever loves an innovation then Allāh will render his actions void and take away *Imān* from his heart. I have hope that Allāh will forgive the (sins of the) individual who has hatred for *Ahl al-Bid*ᶜ*ah*."[16]

Khawajā Muḥammad Maᶜsūm Sirhindī writes in his *Maktūb* [p.110],

> "Oh brother beware of the gatherings of the people of innovation."[17]

These statements highlight the seriousness and the gravity of innovations and one can tell how dangerous they are. Therefore, this obligates every Muslim to abstain and to be aware of innovations. He must strive and continue to learn the definition of innovation in order to correctly recognise them and thereby save himself.[18]

*Majālis al-Abrār wa Masālik al-Akḥyār wa Maḥā'if al-Bid*ᶜ*ah Maqām*ᶜ*e al-Ashrār* for further statements.

[16] Ibn Baṭṭah, *al-Ibānah al-Kubrā* [1:455]. Fuḍail bin Āᶜyyāḍ said, *"When Allāh loves a servant He increases his pain, and when He hates a servant He makes this world wide for him."* Ibn al-Mubārak remarked, *"When Fuḍayl bin Ā*ᶜ*yyāḍ died, sadness passed out of this world."* It is famously reported about him that he was a highway robber until Allāh guided his heart towards the religion. He died in 187H. Fuḍail has many tremendous sayings which have been recorded in the era of the Salaf. One of these sayings is *"Follow the path of guidance and worry not how few are the number of those who are upon it. Leave the paths of misguidance and do not be fooled by the large numbers upon it for they are doomed"* [al-Shāṭibī *al-Ei'tisām* [1:146], Cf. *al-Risālah al-Qushairīyyah* [p.16].

[17] He was Haḍrat Khawāja Imām Muḥammad Maᶜsūm Fārūqī Sirhindī Naqshbandī (d.1668/1079). He is not from the people of knowledge nor is he known as such amongst the Salaf. The Naqshbandī Sūfīs have written about him *"Hazrat Khwaja used to say that all my prayers, whether Farḍ or Nawāfil, are offered over the* ᶜ*Arsh. This great sun of guidance left this mortal world on Saturday 9th Rabī al-Awwal 1079H. In the night before this sad day, a voice was heard in every house of Sirhind that tomorrow morning the Qayyūm of this time will depart from this mortal world to the eternal place."* [cf. Naqshbandi.uk]. Allāh's aid is sought from such words.

[18] There are numerous books on *bid*ᶜ*ah* and its evil effects some of which we have quoted in this treatise and others which include the writings of Muḥammad bin Ṣālih al-ᶜUthaymīn, Ṣālih al-Fawzān, ᶜAbdul Salām al-Burjiss and many others from amongst the contemporary scholars and mentioning all of them here will lengthen the notes.

The Definition of *Bid^c^ah*[19]

In light of the statements of the Messenger of Allāh (ﷺ) we can generally define innovations ie *bid^c^ah* as, **"Inventing or introducing something new into the Dīn."**[20] In some further detail we can say,

[19] ^c^Alī Maḥfūẓ said regarding the technical or Sharī^c^ah meaning of *bid^c^ah*, *"A new way introduced in the Dīn which resembles (aspects) of the Sharī^c^ah which is only practiced in order to exceed in worshipping Allāh."* [^c^Alī Maḥfūẓ, *al-Ibdā^c^ Fī Maḍhār al-Ibtidā^c^* [p.15]

[20] **[A]** The linguistic definition of *bid^c^ah* is: *"Something invented without having any prior example."* This is based upon its usage in the Qur'ān in the saying of Allāh, **"Say: "I am not a new thing *(bid^c^an)* amongst the Messengers" (Sūrah al-Aḥqāf:9)**, meaning Muḥammad is not a new thing amongst the Messengers, as he has precedents and prior examples before him (Isā, Mūsā, Ibrāhīm and so on). [Shāṭibī, *al-Ei^c^tisām* [1:43]. Some linguists have defined *bid^c^ah* as, *"Innovating something new in the Dīn after its completion or any statement or action based on whims, desires or personal opinion innovated after the Messenger of Allāh (ﷺ)."* Some added *"A statement or action without and prior precedence."* [*al-Qāmūs al-Muḥiṭ* [p.906], Ibn Manzūr, *Lisān al-^c^Arab* [6:8], Ibn al-Fāris, *Mu^c^ajam al-Maqā^c^is Fil Lugha* [p.119] and Ibn Taymiyyah, *Fatāwa* [35:414]. **[B]** The word *bid^c^ah* in the Dīn has many meanings attached to it. One such meaning is given by al-Shāṭibī who said, *"Bid^c^ah is an expression of a path taken in the religion, which is invented and resembles the Sharī^c^ah and by whose practice exaggeration in worshipping Allāh is intended"* [Shāṭibī, *al-Ei^c^tisām* [1:53]. Ibn Rajab said. *"Bid^c^ah refers to newly invented actions which have no basis in the Sharī^c^ah. Actions that do have a basis in the Sharī^c^ah are not classed as innovations and are understood in the linguistic sense."* [Ibn Rajab, *Jām^c^e Ulūm al-Ḥikam* [2:127-128]. **[C]** The Scholars of Ahlus Sunnah have explained that innovation is of two types. That which is ***Ḥaqīqīyyah*** *(or ḥaqīqī)*, meaning proper innovation, in every sense of the word. It has absolutely no association to, or basis in the Sharī^c^ah. [Shāṭibī, *al-Ei^c^tisām* [1:367]. It is when a person seeks nearness to Allāh through something the Messenger of Allāh (ﷺ) never sought nearness to Allāh with at all, in its very foundation. From the examples of this type of innovation is seeking nearness to Allāh through celebrating birthdays, through dancing and music, or through acting. Some scholars have mentioned different examples like monasticism and secluding oneself from the worldly life and benefits etc. Such people impose fabrictated types of worship on themselves. [Shāṭibī, *al-Ei^c^tisām* [1:370], Ibn Kathīr, *Tafsīr al-Qur^ɔ^ān al-A^c^ẓīm* [4:316], Sa^c^dī, *Taysīr al-Karīm ar-Rahmān Fī Tafsīr Kalām al-Manān* [1:782]. Shāṭibī mentions numerous other examples in his book. [Shāṭibī, *al-Ei^c^tisām* [1:370-445]. **[D]** As for that which is ***Iḍāfīyyah*** (that which has a basis in the religion), this is when a person seeks nearness to Allāh on account of something by which nearness is in fact sought with Allāh in its foundation (asl).

"Introducing something new into the Dīn which has no evidence from the Messenger of Allāh (ﷺ) or the companions, with the intent of receiving reward and thinking it is his means of salvation by acting on it. (ie the *bidᶜah*)"[21]

Shaikh ul-Islām Imām Ibn Taymiyyah has further elucidated and said, it means to introduce an action, which was not practised during the time of the Messenger of Allāh (ﷺ), and there was no obstacle that prevented them from doing it. Furthermore, there was no legal reason for them to even formulate an innovation, so despite this if a new

However, to which he adds something which takes it away from the form that it came with in the Sharīᶜah and this is done in respect to six matters: **(i)** al-Kam (number), **(ii)** al-Kayf (form), **(iii)** al-Jins (type), **(iv)** al-Ṣabab (cause, reason), **(v)** al-Makān (place), **(vi)** al-Zamān (time). Hence, ***Bidᶜah Iḍāfīyah*** [despite having a basis in the Sharīᶜah] is rejected just as ***Bidᶜah Ḥaqīqīyah*** is. This is because the six matters above are never established in the Qurᵓān and Sunnah when the asal or foundation will be in the Qurᵓān and Sunnah. [Ṣāleḥ bin Saᶜd al-Suḥaimī, *Tanbīyyah Ulil al-Abṣār Ila Kamāl al-Dīn Wa Ma Fī al-Bidᶜah Min Akhṭār* [p.96], ᶜAdawī, *Uṣūl Fī'l Bidᶜah Waᵓl Sunan* [p.30] (also known as *Ṭarīq al-Wuṣūl Ilā Ibṭāl al-Bidᶜah bi ᶜIlm al-Uṣūl*). An example of ***Bidᶜah Iḍāfīyah*** would be to offer special prayers in mid Shaᶜbān despite prayer being established in the Dīn the mode and form of such a prayer is not established by the Messenger of Allāh (ﷺ) at the particular time, hence it is an innovation. Examples of this are making Zikr in unison after the five daily prayers etc. [Shāṭibī, *al-Eiᶜtisām* [1:452], Ṣāleḥ bin Saᶜd al-Suḥaimī, *Tanbīyyah Ulil al-Abṣār Ila Kamāl al-Dīn Wa Ma Fī al-Bidᶜah Min Akhṭār* [p.96]. **[E]** In fact, the ḥadīth of Āᶜishah, *"Whoever introduces something into this affair of ours which does not belong to it, shall have it rejected."* leads to the irrefutable conclusion that, nothing is considered a *bidᶜah* in the *Sharīᶜah* sense except when these conditions are met. These three conditions are: ***'al-Ihdāth'*** - Introducing something new, ***'al-Iḍhāfah'*** - Ascribing it to the religion, ***'A'dm al-Dalīl ash-Sharᶜī'*** - Absence of Sharīᶜah evidence [for this newly-introduced matter] in either a general way or a specific way from the prophet of Allāh. [See also ᶜAlī Nāṣir al-Faqīhi, *al-Bidᶜah Ḍawābiṭha Wa Atharuhā al-Sayyᶜia Fiᶜl Ummah* [p.12-13]. The Albanian Ḥadīth Master, Muḥammad Nāṣir al-Dīn al-Albānī was of the opinion that most innovations are based on general principles which are still impermissible and al-Shatibi classed such innovations as **Iḍāfī**. [al-Albāni, *Ṣaḥīḥ Targīb Waᵓl Tarhīb* [1:54-55], *al-Radd al-Taᶜqīb al-Hathīth* [p.48]

[21] Ibn Taymiyyah said *"An innovation in the Dīn of Islām is every action not legislated by Allāh The Most High nor his Messenger (ﷺ) ie something not legislated which is neither mandatory nor recommended."* [Ibn Taymiyyah, *Majmūᶜa Fatāwa* [4:107-108]

action is performed with the understanding that it is part of the Dīn, then this is an innovation.[22]

The Categories of *Bid^c^ah*[23]

Some people have attempted to save themselves from the punishment the Messenger of Allāh (ﷺ) mentioned for innovations. They have attempted to create a new way by formulating two types of innovations, they say there are two types of *bid^c^ah*, a *Bid^c^ah us-Sayyi^c^a* (evil or bad *bid^c^ah*) and *Bid^c^ah Ḥasanah* (ie a good *bid^c^ah*).[24]

[22] There are numerous statements of Ibn Taymiyyah regarding *bid^c^ah* and its principles. For further clarification of Ibn Taymiyyahs words refer to *Majmū^c^a al-Fatāwa* [4:194, 22:306, 18:346, 35:414]

[23] Some Scholars have categorised *bid^c^ah* in various ways and this categorisation is based on elucidation and clarification and not by rank as in *bid^c^ah ḥasanah* or *sayyi^c^a.* al-Ḥakamī said, *"There are two types of innovations which harm a persons Dīn, (i) A bid^c^ah which takes an individual to the realm of Kufr ie disbelief ie al-Mufakirrah. (ii) A bid^c^ah which does not take a person to the level of Kufr ie disbelief ie Mufassiqah or Ghair Mukaffirah."* An example of *bid^c^ah Mukafirrah* is rejecting something that is definitively established in the Qur^ᵓ^ān or Ḥadīth or vice versa adding something into the Dīn such as making something lawful or unlawful or denying an obligation which is incumbent upon him from Islām. An example of *bid^c^ah Mufassiqah* is one in which the rulings of Islām are not denied or rejected. For example, regularly delaying the prayers or giving the E^c^īd sermon before the prayer. [al-Ḥakamī, *Ma^c^arij al-Qabūl* [2:503-504] from ^c^Alī Nāṣir al-Faqīhi, *al-Bid^c^ah Ḍawābiṭha Wa Atharuhā al-Sayy^c^ia Fi^c^l Ummah* [p.21]. al-Shaṭibī also mentions this categorisation in his *al-Ei^c^tisām* [2:516]. One should note both types are evil and the only difference if whether an individual becomes a disbeliever or not the case of good or bad *bid^c^ah.* ^c^Alī Nāṣir al-Faqīhi further mentions innovations can be categorised into 3 types, (i) Action, (ii) Belief (iii) Statement and then he goes onto explain them with examples. [^c^Alī Nāṣir al-Faqīhi, *al-Bid^c^ah Ḍawābiṭha Wa Atharuhā al-Sayy^c^ia Fi^c^l Ummah* [p.21-24]. Ibn Taymiyyah mentions there are two types of innovations (in) (i) Statements and beliefs (ii) Actions and worship, thus both categories are incorporative and mutually inclusive of each other. [Ibn Taymiyyah, *Majmu^c^a Fatāwa* [22:306]. al-Shāṭibī gives other examples of ***Bid^c^ah Ḥaqīqī*** and ***Bid^c^ah Iḍāfī***.

[24] Some scholars of the past have also made this distinction of good and bad *bid^c^ah* and they include the likes of ^c^Izz al-Dīn bin Abdus Salām, Abū Shāmah and Nawawī. There is also a statement from al-Shāf^c^ī in this regard with a similar menaing as cited by Ibn Ḥajr in his *al-Fatḥ al-Bārī* [13:353] [Izzat Alī ^c^Atiyyah, *al-Bid^c^ah* [pp.197-

So they argue and say, even we do not believe in bad *bid^cahs*, but good *bid^cah's* or *Bid^cah Ḥasanah* is something praiseworthy because they encourage righteous actions, therefore there is no harm in them. This is indeed a major deception which shayṭān has immersed the people of innovation in. In reality there is no basis for this at all.[25]

198]. Such distinctions and categorisations have been oft repeated by the people of innovation and misguidance in order to cause doubt and confusion amongst the Muslims. One of the most prominent figureheads was the Sūfī Barailwī ᶜAbdul Samᶜi Rāmpūrī in his book *Anwār al-Saṭiᶜa* who propounded the idea of good and bad *bidᶜah* and then the latter days Sufi Barailwis propagated this. (Cf. *Anwār al-Saṭiᶜa* [pp.35, 47]. The late Pākistānī Ḥadīth Master, Muḥammad Gondalwī answers this categorisation and says, *"I say this categorisation which has been cited from some of the scholars, then some of them did hold this opinion (ie a good and bad bidᶜah) whereas others disagreed with this categorisation and considered every innovation to be evil and bad. Their difference is a linguistic one, the scholars who uphold this categorisation explain the aforementioned definition as something which had no basis at all during the life of the Messenger of Allāh (ﷺ). So on this basis innovations can be categorised. On the contrary the scholars who also use this definition for bidᶜah and do not believe in this categorisation take the Sharīᶜah meaning and definition of bidᶜah and thus they say anything which has no evidence from the Sharīᶜah regarding its permissibility during he life of the Messenger of Allāh (ﷺ) is an innovation."* He then goes onto cite Mulla ᶜAlī Qārī quoting al-Nawawī as saying, *"Bidᶜah is every action which has no prior example and in the Sharīᶜah it is inventing something new which was not practised during the time of the Messenger of Allāh (ﷺ)."* (Mulla ᶜAlī Qārī, *Mirqāt Sharh Mishkāt* [1:367]. Muḥammad Gondalwī goes onto mention the statement of Ibn Ḥajr al-Haithamī where he said the scholars who categorised *bidᶜah* as good and bad, did so on the basis of its linguistic meaning and the scholars who said every innovation is misguidance took the Sharīᶜah meaning. [Muḥammad Gondalwī, *al-Iṣlaḥ* [2:277-285]

[25] As mentioned the people of innovation and heresy hide behind the general statements of ᶜIzz bin ᶜAbdus Salām in support of good innovations, however he refutes the principles of the people of innovations and says, *"Likewise and similarly praying and fasting everytime and at every instance does not achieve closeness to Allāh this is because sometimes an ignorant person attempts to seek closeness to Allāh with such actions whereas in actual fact they push him further away from him yet they have no idea whatsoever."* [ᶜIzz bin Abdus Salām, *al-Masājalah ᶜIlmīyyah* [p.8]. al-Albānī further said in a clarification note to ᶜIzz bin ᶜAbdus Salāms statement that innovations are of three types, *"This can possibly refer to the linguistic meaning of bidᶜah because of the generalty of the statement of the Messenger of Allāh (ﷺ) that every innovation is misguidance according to the Ḥadīth, "Every bidᶜah is misguidance and every misguidance is in the Fire."* [*Muslim* [no.867], *Nasāᶜi* [no.1579], *Ibn Mājah* [no.45] [al-Albānī's notes to *al-Masājalah ᶜIlmīyyah* [p.3]

The first point to consider is that after reading the statement of the Messenger of Allāh (ﷺ) that every innovation is misguidance, it does not leave any scope for this categorisation, whether they are bad or good innovations. Secondly, the concept of bad *bid^c^ahs* is in itself baseless. When innovations are bad and evil there is no doubt in them being impermissible.

Let us for example assume a proponent of *Bid^c^ah us-Sayyi^c^a* says that bad *bid^c^ahs* refers to music, singing, lewd and shameless behaviour or taking *Riba*. They say how can teaching the people something good and praiseworthy be an innovation. Most people fall into error here because they do not think that music, singing, open evil behaviour and usury are evil actions, which Allāh declared to be sins. Allāh declared them to be unlawful and impermissible based on numerous evidences from the Qur᾿ān and Sunnah. Furthermore, no Muslim commits these acts with the intention of receiving reward. Those who perform these acts are also fully aware of their prohibition and impermissibility in the Sharī^c^ah.

Whereas innovations are done with the aim and intention of seeking reward.[26] These acts and practices in their apparent and general form appear to be good, however, because they have not been established or proven from Messenger of Allāh (ﷺ) or the companions, they have been rendered and considered to be innovations. This vanguard was established in order to prevent the people from introducing and inventing new things in the religion.

For example, let's take an individual who prays two rak^c^ahs of prayer before the E^c^īd prayer.[27] Praying optional prayers is not something bad, in fact it is a good deed. The individual who offers this optional prayer does so in order to seek reward. However, in reality

[26] Ibn Taymīyyah said, *"As for the affairs of the Sharī^c^ah, it is said all aspects of worship are based on Ittibā and not upon innovation. Thus, no individual has the right to do anything in the Dīn which Allāh has not ordered and therefore, it is not permissible for anyone to face the grave of the Messenger of Allāh (ﷺ) whilst praying."* [Ibn Taymīyyah, *Radd ^c^Alal Bakrī* [p.68]

[27] Cf. Is it permissible to pray optional prayers before the E^c^īd Ṣalah [Maḥmūd Aḥmad Mirpūrī, *Fatāwa Ṣirāt al-Mustaqīm* [pp.310-311]

the fact of the matter is that it is an innovation and there is no reward,[28] rather such an individual is sinning because this is something new which was not practised by the Messenger of Allāh (ﷺ).
ᶜAlī (ؓ)[29] prohibited an individual from praying two rakᶜahs before the Eᶜīd prayer. The person said I am only praying and not doing anything bad. ᶜAlī (ؓ) replied.

> "Allāh does not reward an action until the action is practised and established from the Messenger of Allāh (ﷺ). You praying is a sin and meaningless because such actions are unlawful and it may be that Allāh will punish you for opposing his Messenger."[30]

So after this clarification, saying there are good innovations ie *Bidᶜah Ḥasanah*, is total ignorance and a sheer lack of knowledge.[31] Some

[28] There is no prayer before the Eᶜīd prayer. Ibn ᶜAbbās (ؓ) reported, *"The Messenger of Allāh (ﷺ) went out (to the musallah) on the Day of Fitr and prayed two rakᶜahs (of Eid prayer), not praying before or after them."* [*Bukhārī, Muslim* and others [*Irwā ul-Ghalīl* [no.631]. Ibn Ḥajr said, *"Ibn al-Aᶜrabī said, "If praying voluntary prayers in the musalla was practiced (by the Ṣaḥābah), it would have been reported to us. Those who permit it do so because that time is an open time for prayer. And those who avoid it do so because the Messenger of Allāh (ﷺ) did not do it. "And whoever follows the example (of the Prophet) is guided." Therefore, there is no confirmed voluntary prayer before or after the Eid prayer – contrary to those who liken it to the Jumuᶜah prayer."* [Ibn Ḥajr, *Fatḥ al-Bārī* [2:614].

[29] He is ᶜAlī ibn Abī Ṭālib ibn ᶜAbd al-Muṭṭalib bin Hāshim bin ᶜAbd Manāf bin Qusay bin Kilāb bin Murrah bin Kaᶜb (ؓ). Born on 23 BH (13th Rajab) (Makkah). ᶜAlī (ؓ) was the only person born in the Kaᶜba sanctuary in Makkah, the holiest place in Islām. His father was Abū Ṭālib ibn ᶜAbd al-Muṭṭalib (Quraishī) and his mother was Fātima bint Asad but he was raised in the household of Muḥammad (ﷺ), who himself was raised by Abū Ṭālib, Muḥammad's (ﷺ) uncle. When the Messenger of Allāh (ﷺ) reported receiving a divine revelation, ᶜAlī (ؓ) was among the first to accept his message, dedicating his life to the cause of Islām. The fourth Kaliph of the Muslims who was martyred on 21 Ramaḍān 40H in Kūfā. There are 95 narrations from him in Bukhārī and 51 in Muslim. [*al-Iṣābah* [2:105], *Tārīkh āl-Kabīr* [6:259], *Ṭabaqāt* [9:137], *Tahdhīb al-Tahdhīb* [7:334 no.565]. *Taqrīb at-Tahdhīb* [2:39], *Asad al-Ghābah* [4:91], *al-Ḥilyah* [2:87], *Shadhrāt al-Dhahab* [1:49], *Tārīkh as-Saghīr* [1:435], *al-Jarḥ* [6:191], *Tārīkh Baghdād* [1:133].

[30] *al-Bināyah Sharḥ al-Hidāyah* [3:105].

[31] There are also many sayings of the Salaf concerning *bidᶜah* being evil and even if the people think it something praiseworthy. Some sayings follow, **[A]** ᶜAbd Allāh ibn

people also put forth the statement of ᶜUmar (ﷺ)[32] when he started the congregation for *Tarāwīḥ* prayer he said, *"This is a good bidᶜah."*[33]

Masᶜūd (ﷺ) said *"Follow (the Sunnah) and do not innovate, for you have been given that which is sufficient and every innovation is misguidance"* [Abū Khaithamah, *Kitāb ul-ᶜIlm* [no.54] graded Ṣaḥīḥ by al-Albānī]. **[B]** Hudhayfah ibn al-Yamān (ﷺ) said, *"Every act of worship which the Companions did not do, do not do it."* [Shāṭibī, *al-Eiᶜtisām* [1:418] also *Amr bil Ittiba Wa Nahi al-Ibtibā* by Suyūṭī [p.3], authenticated by al-Albānī in *Ḥujjat Nabī* [1:100] and *Manāsik Ḥajj* [1:44]. **[C]** ᶜAbd Allāh ibn ᶜUmar (ﷺ) said *"Every Innovation is Misguidance, even if the people consider it to be something good."* [Lālikāᶜi, *Sharḥ Usūl al-Eiᶜtiqād* [no.126], al-Baihaqī, *al-Madkhal Ilas-Sunan* [no.191], Ibn Naṣr, *as-Sunnah* [p.24], Its isnād (chain of narration) is Ṣaḥīḥ]. **[D]** ᶜAbd Allāh ibn Masᶜūd (ﷺ) said, *"Moderation upon the Sunnah is better than exertion in innovation."* [Suyūṭī, *al-Amr bil Ittibā Wan Nahi Anil-Ibtidā'*[1:2)] **[E]** Abuᵓl-Āᶜlīyah said, *"You must stick to the original state of affairs which they were upon, before they are divided."* [*al-Amr bil-'Ittibaa wan-Nahi ᶜAnil Ibtidā* [1:2]. **[F]** Imām az-Zuhrī said, *"The people of knowledge who came before us used to say, "Salvation lies in clinging to the Sunnah."* [al-Dārimī [no.96], Ṣaḥīḥ, Fawāz Aḥmad]. **[G]** ᶜAbd Allāh Ibn ᶜUmar (ﷺ) said, *"Every innovation is misguidance, even if the people see it as something good."* [al-Dārimī, *Abū Shāmah* [no.39], Ibn Naṣr, *as-Sunnah* [no.82], al-Lālikāᶜī, *Sharḥ Usūl al-Eiᶜtiqād* [1:92 no.126], al-Baihaqī in *al-Madkhal* [no.191]. It was authenticated by al-Albānī, *Aḥkām al-Janā'iz* [no.258] and *Iṣlah al-Masājid* [no.13]. Salīm al-Ḥilāli said, *"Its isnād (chain of narration) is as authentic as the sun!"* **[H]** ᶜAbd Allāh Ibn Masᶜūd (ﷺ) said, "Moderation in applying Sunnah is better than striving hard in following *bidᶜah*." [Ṭabarānī, *al-Mu'ajam al-Kabīr* [10:208].

[32] He is Umar bin al-Khattab bin Nufayl bin ᶜAbdul ᶜUzza bin Riyah bin ᶜAbd Allāh bin Qurt bin Razah bin ᶜAdi bin Kaᶜb. In the beginning of Prophethood, Muslims were few and weak. Allāh guided ᶜUmar bin al-Khaṭṭāb (ﷺ) to serve Islām. ᶜUmar bin al-Khaṭṭāb (ﷺ) was a great pillar of strength for Islām. Umar bin al-Khattāb had great virtue and was also very pious and sincere. He used to cry during his Ṣalah! On one occasion the Messenger of Allāh (ﷺ) said to ᶜUmar (ﷺ) *"By Allāh, Shayṭān will never tread the way you pass through."* He was martyred in Madīnah in the year 23H. He has 95 narrations in Bukhārī and in Muslim 43. [*al-Isābah* [4:589-591], *Tārīkh al-Kābīr* [6:49], *Tahdhīb al-Tahdhīb* [7:441 no.725]. *Taqrīb at-Tahdhīb* [2:54], *Khulaṣah Tahdhīb al-Kamāl* [2:268], *al-Kāshif* [2:309], *al-Thiqāt* [8:447].

[33] Ṣaḥīḥ al-Bukhārī [no.227]. In fact according to one view even Imām Abū Ḥanīfah said the words of ᶜUmar are not to be seen him introducing a *bidᶜah* in the Dīn. Ibn Āᶜbidīn [1252H] said that it was mentioned in *al-Ikhtiyār* (a Ḥanafī book of fiqh) that Abū Yūsuf asked Abū Ḥanīfah about ᶜUmar's action and Abū Ḥanīfah responded back by saying that *"Tarāwīḥ is a Sunnah Mu'akkadah and that Umar didn't do it from his own self as an innovator, for the foundation of his action is from the Messenger of Allāh (ﷺ)"* [*Radd al-Mukhtār ᶜAla Durr al-Mukhtār* [1:169]. **[A]** al-ᶜUthaymīn said

We shall discuss this in detail and at length whether praying *Tarāwīḥ* prayer in congregation is an innovation or not. It should suffice to say that ᶜUmar (ﷺ) did not take or mean the *Sharīᶜah* definition of the word *bidᶜah* but rather he used its linguistic meaning. In doing so, he restarted something which had been abandoned and when he restarted it, he used the words, *'this is good bidᶜah'*.

This does not mean at all that ᶜUmar (ﷺ) started something new in the Dīn with the intention of seeking reward. In addition, this was not something new because the Messenger of Allāh (ﷺ) had established the *Tarāwīḥ* prayer in congregation himself. So how can this be an innovation? Therefore, anything that is invented or something that is started new in the Dīn, thinking that it is rewarding, is an innovation and indeed they are all evil.

concerning this narration, *"Thus performing the night prayer in Ramadhan as a single* jama'ah *is from the* sunnah *of the Messenger (ﷺ), and ᶜUmar, (ﷺ), referred to it as a bidᶜah* considering *the fact that after the Messenger of Allāh (ﷺ) had left leading the prayer, the people became separated such that one person would he praying alone, and elsewhere two would be praying together, and somewhere else three would be praying in* jamāᶜah. *So throughout the mosque there were people praying alone and in groups, so ᶜUmar, the chief of the Believers, had the idea - and this idea was perfectly correct - to gather the people to pray behind a* single *Imām. So this action was an innovation in the sense that it was new and different to how the people were before, i.e., praying in separate groups. Hence this bidᶜah was relative and subjective - not original and absolute, being set up by ᶜUmar (ﷺ), as this* Sunnah *was there during the time of the Messenger of Allāh (ﷺ). So it indeed was a* Sunnah *(not a bidᶜah), which had been abandoned since the time of the Messenger of Allāh (ﷺ), until ᶜUmar (ﷺ), revived it."* [al-ᶜUthaymīn, *Bidᶜah - The Unique Nature of the Perfection found in Islām and the Grave Danger of Innovating in to it*, [pp.11-20]. **[B]** Ibn Kathīr said in his Tafsīr that: *"There are two types of bidᶜah, religious, as mentioned in the Ḥadīth: "Every innovation is a bidᶜah and every bidᶜah is heresy." And there is a linguistic bidᶜah, such as the statement of the Leader of the faithful ᶜUmar bin al-Khaṭṭāb when he gathered the Muslims to pray the Tarāwīḥ prayer in congregation (which was also an earlier practice of the* Messenger of Allāh (ﷺ)*) and said, "What a good bidᶜah this is."* [Ibn Kathīr, *Tafsīr Qurʾān al-Aᶜẓīm* Sūrah al-Baqarah:117].

Whenever an Innovation is Introduced a Sunnah is Lost

So whenever an innovation is introduced, a Sunnah is lost and this was prophesised by the most truthful, the Messenger of Allāh (ﷺ) and this has been witnessed on numerous occasions. Whenever something new is invented in the religion, which did not exist nor did it have any basis in the best three generations, we see that the Sunnah is abandoned. Important and well known Sunnahs are abandoned and not practised. In this regard the following two aḥadīth elucidate this meaning. Guḍaif bin Ḥārith Thumālī (ﷺ) narrates the Messenger of Allāh (ﷺ) said,

> "When a nation practices an innovation, a Sunnah like it is taken away from them, therefore, hold firmly onto the Sunnah which is better than innovation."[34]

The second ḥadīth is from *al-Dārimī* in which Ḥassān narrates the Messenger of Allāh (ﷺ) said,

> "The nation that introduces an innovation into the Dīn, then Allāh will take away its like from their Sunnah from them and it will not be returned to them until the day of judgement." [*al-Dārimī*][35]

[34] Aḥmad, *Musnad* [28:172 no.16970], Ibn Qānᶜe, *Muᶜajam as-Ṣahābah* [2:316], Marwazī, *as-Sunnah* [p.27], Abū Ḥafs Bazzār, *Musnad* [no.131], Ṭabarānī, *Muᶜajam al-Kabīr* [18:178], Abū Zurᶜah, *Tārīkh* [1:603-604], Haithamī, *al-Majmāᶜa al-Zawāʾid* [1:188].

[35] al-Dārimī, *Sunan* [1:35 no.98], Ibn al-Waḍḍah, *al-Bidᶜah* [2:80 no.90], Ibn Baṭṭah, *al-Ibānah* [1:351 no.228], Lālikāᶜī, *Sharḥ Usūl al-Eiᶜtiqād* [1:104 no.129], Abū Nuᶜaym, *al-Ḥilyah* [6:73]. al-Albānī graded it *Ṣaḥīḥ* (authentic) in *al-Mishkāt* [1:66 no.188]. Various other similar reports are recorded such as, Ibn ᶜAbbās (ﷺ) said, *"Not a year passes by except that people invent an innovation and kill a Sunnah, until innovation will remain and Sunnah will die."* [*al-Muᶜjam al-Kabīr* 10:262 no.10610]. Ibn Sīrīn said, *"No practices an innovation except that he removes a Sunnah (through it)."* [*al-Dārimī* [no.210], al-Barbahāri said, *"Know that people have never invented an innovation, except that they have abandoned a similar Sunnah."* [al-Barbahārī, *Sharḥ as-Sunnah* [p.68].

These are the sayings of the noble Messenger (ﷺ), doubting his statements are tantamount to disbelief. However, when we look at society where innovations are widespread,[36] the truthfulness and honesty of the words of the Messenger of Allāh (ﷺ) become a stark reality. We will discuss this later in more detail but we shall present two examples here.

The supplications and invocations the Messenger of Allāh (ﷺ) used to recite after the obligatory prayers are well documented in all of the books of Ḥadīth. They mention that he would say *Allāhu Akbar* loudly once and then *Astagfirullāh* 3 times, he would recite Āyah al-Kursī and then say *SubḥanAllāh* 33 times, *Alḥamdulillāh* 33 times and then *Allāhu Akbar* 34 times. Alternatively reciting all three praises 33 times each and following it with the *praise La Ilaha IllAllāhu Wahdahu La Sharikalahu Lahulmulku Wala Hulhamdu Wa Huwa ᶜAla Kulli Shayᵓin Qadīr.*

However nowadays you will find most of the worshippers reciting *La Ilaha Illal Allāh* loudly (and also in unison)[37] followed by saying

[36] Hudaifah bin al-Yamān (رضي الله عنه) said, *"Wallāhi, innovations will become so widespread so much so that if they are abandoned the people will say you have abandoned a Sunnah."* [Ibn Waḍḍah, *Kitāb Fiha Mā Jā Fi'l Bidᶜah* [no.162, p.124]

[37] Cf. previous footnotes regarding ***Bidᶜah Iḍāfīyah*** for how something may seem to have a basis in the Sharᶜīah but despite this it will be rejected. As for modern day Sūfīs and others performing Zikr aloud after the prayers and in groups then this is an innovation. In some countries they play musical instruments with there so called Zikr. The scholars of the Standing Committee said, *"Zikr in unison is an innovation (Bid'ah) because it is something that has been introduced into the religion. The Messenger of Allāh (ﷺ) said: "Whoever introduces something into this matter of ours that is not part of it will have it rejected." And he (ﷺ) said: "Every newly invented matter is an innovation, and every innovation is going astray." What is prescribed is to remember Allāh, may He be exalted, without reciting in unison."* [*Fatāwa al-Lajnah al-Dāᶜimah*, [24:268]. It is more makrūh (disliked) to raise the voice in reciting Zikr and duᶜā and to recite in unison, if that could annoy other people who are praying or offering duᶜā or remembering Allāh (Zikr). It was narrated from ᶜAbd Allāh ibn ᶜUmar (رضي الله عنه) that the Messenger of Allāh (ﷺ) observed Iᶜtikāf and addressed the people, saying: *"When one of you stands to pray, he is conversing with his Lord, so let each of you think of what he is saying to his Lord, and no one among you should raise his voice over anyone else when reciting in the prayer."* [*Aḥmad* [no.4909] classed as *Ṣaḥīḥ* by al-Albānī.] Ibn Taymiyyah said, *"No one should raise his voice in recitation in such a way that he annoys others, such as other worshippers."* [Ibn Taymiyyah,

Muhammad ar-Rasūlullāh once and then they begin to pray the Sunnah prayers or some of them begin to recite the salutations.

The issue is that on the face of it, these recitations are praiseworthy but why have the supplications and invocation of the Messenger of Allāh (ﷺ) been abandoned? When something new is introduced, most of the Muslims are not even aware or have any knowledge of the recommended supplications and invocations. We know this is something the Muslims formulated themselves and gave it a particular image and presentation, so much so that most of the Muslims are negligent of the Sunnah of the Messenger of Allāh (ﷺ) and what he taught the companions.

Majmūᶜ al-Fatāwa [23:61]. With regard to the report narrated by *Muslim* [no.2701] from Muᶜāwīyah ibn Abī Sufyān (ؓ) according to which the Messenger of Allāh (ﷺ) came out to a circle of his companions and said, *"Why are you sitting here?" They said: We are sitting to remember Allāh and praise Him for having guided us to Islām and blessed us with it. He said: "By Allāh, are you only sitting for that purpose? They said: By Allāh, we are only sitting for that purpose. He said: "I did not ask you to swear because I am accusing you, but Jibrā'īl came to me and told me that Allāh was boasting of you to the Angels." And the report also narrated by Muslim [no.2699) from Abu Hurairah (ؓ) who said: The Messenger of Allāh (ﷺ) said: "No people gather in one of the houses of Allāh, reciting the Book of Allāh and studying it together, but tranquillity will descend upon them, mercy will overshadow them, the angels will surround them and Allāh will mention them to those who are with Him."* There is nothing in these reports to suggest that Zikr should be recited in unison. Ibn ᶜUthaymīn said, *"The correct view concerning this matter is that the two ḥadīths refer to those who study the Book of Allāh together and recite it. Similarly, with regard to people who are remembering Allāh, it is general in meaning and should be understood in the light of other, specific reports that describe the way in which Zikr was done at the time of the Messenger of Allāh (ﷺ) and his Companions. It was not known among them that they would remember Allāh, may He be exalted, by reciting Zikr in unison or that they read or recited the Qurʾān in unison. The phrase "studying it together" indicates that this studying together is done one after another. Either one reads, and when he has finished the next one reads the same text, and so on; or each one of them reads one part, and the next one reads from where the first one stopped. This is the apparent meaning of the hadeeth. With regard to the other hadeeth in which it says that they remembered Allāh, we say the same thing: it is general in meaning and should be understood in the light of the texts that speak of the specific way in which Zikr was done at the time of the Messenger of Allāh (ﷺ) and his Companions. It was not known among them that they would get together and recite Zikr in unison."* [Ibn al-ᶜUthaymīn, *Fatāwa Nūr ᶜAla al-Ḍarb* [19:30].

Another example is the occasion of the birth of a child. In light of the statements of the Messenger of Allāh (ﷺ), the Muslims should do *khitnah*, cut the hair after 7 days, name the child, offer *ᶜAqīqah*[38] and then offer charity according to the weight of the child's hair. However when we ponder on the current situation of the Muslims we find a handful of Muslims who offer the Sunnah[39] of *ᶜAqīqah.*[40]

We rather find instead that they distribute Asian sweets as well as other gifts but yet fail to return to the Sunnah. I do not mean that distributing Asian sweets is impermissible but if a Sunnah is abandoned and side-lined and something else is adopted and considered to be obligatory or is promoted and propagated among the masses, then this is something that is impermissible. This is because for a Muslim, the Sunnah of the Messenger of Allāh (ﷺ) should be loved and have priority and precedence over everything. In the same instance, giving charity according to the weight of the child's hair has also been abandoned. In fact, some extremely ignorant individuals instead of following and adopting this Sunnah, present the hair as a sacrificial offering at tombs and shrines.

[38] ᶜAqīqah is a blessed Sunnah which is slowly being forgotten. Narrated Salmān bin ᶜAmir al-Dabbī (رضي الله عنه), *"I heard Allāh's Messenger (ﷺ) saying: "ᶜAqiqah is to be offered for a (newly born) boy, so slaughter (an animal) for him, and relieve him of his suffering."* [*Ṣaḥīḥ Bukhārī* [no.5472]. Unfortunately, early Ḥanafī madhabists completely ignored this practice as Sunnah and it is certainly not proven so from Imām Abū Ḥanīfah. In fact, the view of the Ḥanafī madhab is that: "[no.809] "Muḥammad [the foremost student of Abū Ḥanīfah] said, *"Abū Ḥanīfah informed us from Ḥammād that Ibrāhīm said, "There used to be Āqīqah in the Jāhilīyah, but when Islām came, it was rejected"* [no.810] Muḥammad said, *"Abū Ḥanīfah informed us saying, "A man narrated to us from Muḥammad ibn al-Ḥanafīyyah that there used to be ᶜAqīqah in the Jāhilīyah but when Islām came it was rejected." Muḥammad said, "We adhere to this and it is the verdict of Abu Hanīfah, may Allāh (exalted is He) have mercy on him"* [*Kitāb al Āthār* of Abū Ḥanīfah, English translation by Abdus Samad Clarke [p.477]. Due to ᶜAqīqah not being established from the Ḥanafī Imāms, their madhab says Islām came to reject the ᶜAqīqah yet the blessed Sunnah of the Messenger of Allāh (ﷺ) is in clear contradiction to this. So whose Sunnah will we follow? Abū Ḥanīfah's or the Messenger of Allāh (ﷺ)? Allāh's aid is sought.

[39] Cf.ᶜAqīqah is Sunnah, [Maḥmūd Aḥmad Mirpūrī, *Fatāwa Ṣirāt al-Mustaqīm* [pp.422-424]

[40] Sacrificing 1 or 2 sheep on the occasional of a childs birth.

There are numerous innovations prevalent in our times concerning the mother and child when they give birth. They consider these innovations to be obligatory when they have no basis whatsoever in the Sunnah of the Messenger of Allāh (ﷺ) and this eventually leads to the abandoning the Sunnah and acting upon it.

The Characteristics of Innovations

Innovations have a characteristic, which allows them to be identified very easily. This is because innovations cannot remain in the same state and rather they continuously change, adapt and take on new additions.[41] For example, in the beginning candles were only lit at graves, then sacrificial garments started being placed over graves in tombs and shrines. Then the innovation of washing graves at the shrines started. Then singing and dancing around these graves, tombs and mausoleums started which then changed into fun fairs, festivals and public gatherings.[42] In this era how many shrines and tombs are

---

[41] ᶜAbdul ᶜAzīz ibn ᶜAbd Allāh ibn Bāz said, *"The Salaf warned against innovations because they are additions in the Dīn and an attempt to legislate something new in the Shariᶜah for which Allah and his Messenger (ﷺ) did not give permission and rather this resembles the Yahūd and Nasārah who innovated and introduced new things into their religions."* [ᶜAbdul ᶜAzīz ibn ᶜAbd Allāh ibn Bāz, *Taḥzīr Mina᾽l Bidᶜāh* [p.19]

[42] Visiting shrines, sitting at them, erecting buildings upon them and taking them as places of worship are all forbidden. Jābir (ؓ) narrates that the Messenger of Allāh (ﷺ) *"Forbid us from making structures on the graves, raising them and to sit at them [seeking a blessing]."* [*Muslim* [1:312], Aḥmad, *Musnad* [3:295], Ibn Ḥibbān, *Ṣaḥīḥ Ibn Ḥibbān* [no:3154]. Refer to the excellent book on this topic by Shawkānī entitled *'Sharḥ us-Sudūr Fī Taḥrīm Raf ul-Qabūr.'* In fact, those who blindly follow Abū Ḥanīfah should consider their Imām's verdict on this issues. Muḥammad Shaybānī said *"We say it is impermissible to place extra soil over and above what the grave has in terms of being along the ground and that buildings be erected above the grave and this is what I and Abū Ḥanīfah are upon."* [Muḥammad al-Shaybānī, *Kitāb ul-Āthār* [p.49]. [Cf. al-Albānī's *Taḥzīr al-Sājid Min Itikhāz al-Qubūr Masājid*, Muḥammad Aᶜṭāullāh Ḥanīf al-Bhojiyānī, *Islām And the Veneration of Graves – Contemplation For the Muslims* and *Demolishing Graves* see http://www.salafiri.com/ebook-demolishing-graves/

there, where people prostrate, make *Tawāf* and ask also them for help. We fear the new additions that will take place.[43]

Similarly, and likewise the day of the birth of the Messenger of Allāh (ﷺ) has led many customary practices being innovated in the Dīn. There is no evidence for them from the Messenger of Allāh (ﷺ), from the companions, the *Ahlul Bayt* and the pious predecessors. The founder and the one who formulated the Milād[44] was Sulṭān Mālik

[43] All such acts emanate by imitating the kufār and the companions in the early days of Islām asked the Messenger of Allāh (ﷺ) to single out a tree to resemble the polytheists in seeking tabarruk from it. This is also the affair of most of the Muslims today who imitate and copy the kufār in affairs of innovatins and polytheism and have formulated birthday fesivals of Saints and holy people, introduced innovations during funerals and began to make structures over graves. There is no doubt that imitating the nations before is a means of opening the doors to innovations and abhorent desires. [Cf. al-Fawzān, *Kitāb al-Tawḥīd* [p.87], Ṣāleḥ ibn Saᶜd al-Suḥaimī, *Tanbīyyah Ulil al-Abṣār Ila Kamāl al-Dīn Wa Ma Fī al-Bidᶜah Min Akhṭār* [p.147], Nāṣir al-Aᶜql, *Rasa'il Wa Dirāsāt Fi'l Ahwā Wa'l Iftirāq Wa'l Bidᶜah Wa Mawquf al-Salaf Minhā* [2:150]

[44] In summary the Mawlid was introduced by the Shīᶜa Fātimids after the three best centuries, in order to corrupt the religion of the Muslims. The first person to do this after them was the king al-Muẓaffar Abū Saᶜīd Kaukabūri, the king of Irbil, at the end of the sixth century AH, as mentioned by the historians such as Ibn Khalkān and others. Abū Shāmah said, *"The first person to do that in Mosul was Shaikh ᶜUmar ibn Muḥammad al-Malā, one of the well-known righteous people."* [Abū Shāmah, *al-Bā'ith ᶜA'la Inkār al-Bidᶜah Wal-Ḥawādith* [p.44] Then the ruler of Irbil and others followed his example. Ibn Kathīr said in his biography of Abu Saᶜīd Kaukabūri, *"He used to observe the Mawlid in Rabiᶜ al-Awwal and hold a huge celebration on that occasion... some of those who were present at the feast of al-Muẓaffar on some occasions of the Mawlid said that he used to offer in the feast five thousand grilled heads of sheep, ten thousand chickens and one hundred thousand large dishes, and thirty trays of sweets... he would let the Sufis sing from Zuhr until Fajr, and he himself would dance with them."* [Ibn Kathīr, *al-Bidāyah wa'l Nihāyah* [13:137].

Ibn Khalkān said, *"When it is the first of Safar they decorate those domes with various kinds of fancy adornments, and in every dome there sits a group of singers and a group of puppeteers and players of musical instruments, and they do not leave any one of those domes without setting up a group (of performers) there. The people give up work during this period, and they do no work except going around and watching the entertainment. When there are two days to go until the Mawlid, they bring out a large number of camels, cows and sheep, more than can be described, and they accompany them with all the drums, songs and musical instruments that they have, until they bring them to the square... On the night of the Mawlid there are performances of nashīd after Maghrib in the citadel."* [Ibn Khalkān, *Wafyāt al-Aᶜyān*

[3:274]. This is the origin of this celebration on the occasion of the Prophet's birthday. More recently idle entertainment, extravagance, and wasting of money and time have become associated with an innovation for which Allāh has not sent down any authority.

al-Fawzān said, *"We say to them that reading the biography of the Prophet (ﷺ) and following his example are required of the Muslim all the time, all year long and throughout his life. Singling out a specific day for that with no evidence for doing so is an innovation, and every innovation is a going astray." [Aḥmad [4:164], al-Tirmidhī [no.2676]. Bid^c ah does not bear any fruit but evil and it leads to a person distancing himself from the Prophet (ﷺ). In conclusion, celebrating the birthday of the Prophet (ﷺ) whatever form it takes, is a reprehensible innovation. The Muslims should put a stop to this and other kinds of bid^c ah, and occupy themselves with reviving and adhering to the Sunnah. They should not be deceived by those who promote and defend this bid^c ah, for these types of people are more interested in keeping innovations alive than in reviving the Sunnah; they may not even care about the Sunnah at all. Whoever is like this, it is not permissible to imitate him or follow his example, even if the majority of people are like this. Rather we should follow the example of those who follow the path of the Sunnah, among the righteous Salaf and their followers, even if they are few. Truth is not measured by the men who speak it, rather men are measured by the truth. The Messenger of Allāh (ﷺ) said: "Whoever among you lives (for a long time) will see many differences. I urge you to follow my Sunnah and the way of the rightly-guided khalīfahs who come after me. Hold on to it firmly. Beware of newly-invented matters, for every innovation is a going astray." [Aḥmad [4:126], al-Tirmidhī [no. 2676]. So the Messenger of Allāh (ﷺ) explained to us in this ḥadīth what we should do when there are differences of opinion, just as he explained that everything that goes against his Sunnah, be it words or deeds, is a bid^c ah, and every bid^c ah is a going astray. If we see that there is no basis for celebrating the birthday of the Messenger of Allāh (ﷺ), whether in the Sunnah of the Messenger of Allāh (ﷺ) or in the way of the rightly-guided khalīfahs, then it is one of the newly-invented matters, one of the bid^c ahs which lead people astray. This principle is what is implied by this ḥadīth and is what is indicated by the āyah,* ***"O you who believe! Obey Allāh and obey the Messenger (Muḥammad), and those of you (Muslims) who are in authority. (And) if you differ in anything amongst yourselves, refer it to Allāh and His Messenger, if you believe in Allāh and in the Last Day. That is better and more suitable for final determination."*** *[al-Nisā:59]. Referring to Allāh means referring to His Book, and referring to the Messenger (ﷺ) means referring to his Sunnah after he has passed away. The Qur'ān and Sunnah are the reference point in cases of dispute. Where in the Qur'ān or Sunnah does it indicate that it is prescribed in Islām to celebrate the* Messenger of Allāh's (ﷺ) *birthday? Whoever does that or thinks that it is good must repent to Allāh from this and from other kinds of bid^c ah. This is the attitude of the Muslim who is seeking the truth. But whoever is too stubborn and arrogant after proof has been established, then his reckoning will be with his Lord."* [al-Fawzān, *Huqūq al-Nabī Bayna al-Ijlāl wal-Ikhlāl*

Shāh Seljuqī who orchestrated and organised the first gathering of Milād[45] in the year 485H in Baghdād. So this is not the Sunnah of the Messenger of Allāh (ﷺ) nor the practise of the companions but rather this is the Sunnah of Mālik Shāh.[46]

It is also important to mention as far as the *Sīrah* of the Messenger of Allāh (ﷺ) is concerned and his way of giving daᶜwah, not only was this the best way but it is also obligatory upon every Muslim to spread his teachings and his *Sīrah* everywhere. This will increase and raise the fervour of a Muslim to follow and obey the Messenger of Allāh (ﷺ). However, restricting his teachings and Sīrah to one particular day or date is incorrect.

This is like saying we can only denote a few days to state the love and stature of the Messenger of Allāh (ﷺ) and this is indeed injustice. The individual, who millions upon millions praise and venerate on a

[p.139]. Some scholars have alluded the ascription of Fatimids is incorrect and false because they were in reality jewish, fireworshippers and heretics without any Dīn. [Alī Maḥfūẓ, *al-Ibdāᶜ Fī Maḍār al-Ibtidāᶜ* [p.261], al-Judaīᶜ, *al-Tabarruk Anwāᶜahu Wa Aḥkāmuhu* [pp.359-373], Ṣāleḥ ibn Saᶜd al-Suḥaimī, *Tanbīyyah Ulil al-Abṣār Ila Kamāl al-Dīn Wa Ma Fī al-Bidᶜah Min Akhṭār* [p.232]. Celebrating the birthday of the Messenger of Allāh (ﷺ) resembles the practices and actions of the jews and Christians, which we have been warned from imitating (ie making taqlīd of) them. [Ibn Taymiyyah, *Iqtiḍā al-Ṣirāṭ al-Mustaqīm Li Mukhālifah Aṣhāb al-Jaḥīm* [2:614-615], Ibn Qayyim, *Zād al-Maᶜād* [1:59].

45 We have compiled a series of articles on the innovation of Milād which are still ongoing and the avid reader is requested to refer to the Mawlid Papers on *www.salafiri.com* for further reading.

46 ᶜAbdul ᶜAzīz ibn ᶜAbd Allāh ibn Bāz said, *"To celebrate the anniversary of the birth of Messenger of Allāh (ﷺ) and the others, means that the religion is not perfected by Allāh for this Ummah, and the Messenger (ﷺ) did not impart to the people what was necessary regarding their religious duties, till these late ones appeared and invented in the religion what is not permitted by Allāh, thinking that this would bring them nearer to Allāh. Undoubtedly, this is a great danger and is tantamount to criticizing Allāh the Almighty and the Messenger of Allāh (ﷺ) whereas Allāh the Almighty has already completed the religion and perfected His Grace, and the Messenger of Allāh (ﷺ) has conveyed the Message openly and informed the Ummah of all such ways that will lead them to the Paradise and save them from Hell-fire."* [ᶜAbdul ᶜAzīz ibn ᶜAbd Allāh ibn Bāz, *Wūjūb Lazūm al-Sunnah Waᵓl Ḥazr Minaᵓl Bidᶜah* [p.7]. Cf. ᶜAbdul ᶜAzīz ibn ᶜAbd Allāh ibn Bāz's *Wūjūb al-ᶜAmal Bil-Sunnah al-Nabawīyyah Wa Kufr Man Ankarahā* and *Taḥzīr Minaᵓ Bidᶜah* .]

daily basis in their prayers and salutations. This is the why Allāh, the Creator testified to his grandeur and rank and said,

وَرَفَعْنَا لَكَ ذِكْرَكَ ﴿٤﴾

"And raised high for you your repute."[47]

Who would defy or have the power to oppose this veneration of Allāh. Unfortunately, the Muslims have also engrossed themselves in innovations at this point. They organise special gatherings in the month of Rab^{c}i ul-Awwal and delude themselves into thinking they have shown their love and veneration for the Messenger of Allāh (ﷺ) and fulfilled their rights. In the chaos and false celebrations over these few days, they think they have loved the Messenger of Allāh (ﷺ) yet on the contrary during the remainder of the year they live their lives in total opposition to the teachings and example of the Messenger of Allāh (ﷺ). It seems like they attempt to redeem themselves from their sins in these few days of celebration in the month of Rab^{c}i ul-Awwal.

Their speakers and callers are also responsible for this outcome, who openly misquote and misinterpret narrations and stories from the pulpits and stages in order to justify these celebration.[48] They

[47] Sūrah al-Nashrah:4.

[48] In reality these callers of misguidance were warned against by the he Messenger of Allah (ﷺ) in a Ḥadīth from Ḥudaifah ibn al-Yamān (رضي الله عنه) that the The Messenger of Allah (ﷺ) said that evil will appear, until there appears callers to the gates of hell-fire, and that whoever responds to their call will be thrown by them in the fire *"They (i.e. these callers to the gates of hell-fire) will be from our own people and will speak our language."* [*Bukhārī* [no.7084], *Muslim* [no.1847]. This ḥadīth is a clear warning from the Khawārij and all those people of *shirk* and *bid^{c}ah* who are misguiding the Ummah. al-Nawawī said in explanation of the aforementioned Ḥadīth, *"The scholars said this refers to the leaders who call to innovations and misguidance like the Khawārij, Qaramatah and all those who cause tribulations. This Ḥadīth is an evidence for the obligation and necessity to hold onto the Jamā^{c}ah of the Muslims and their leaders even if they openly commit sin and evil deeds."* (Nawawī, *Sharḥ Ṣaḥīḥ Muslim* [12:237]. al-Fawzān commented on this ḥadīth saying, *"They possess eloquence that grabs the attention of the listener. The listener listens to them because of their eloquent speech. The Messenger of Allah (ﷺ) said, "Indeed some eloquent speech has the influence of magic" (e.g. some people refuse to do something and then a good eloquent speaker addresses them and then they agree to do that very thing after his*

incorrectly try to prove the importance of organising gatherings for *mawlid*, organising conferences, participating in them,[49] encouraging the women to make all kind of food and to distribute it, thereby indoctrinating the people making them think that such actions are the only way to salvation.[50] When the simple minded people listen to these incorrectly interpolated narrations and stories, it increases their fervour to celebrate the birthday of the Messenger of Allāh (ﷺ) vehemently to such an extent that they do not exert the same level of effort in the daily obligatory actions ie the prayer, fasting, Zakāh and Ḥajj etc. These people extend matters and begin to detest the people who do not promote or participate in such gatherings, more so than the people who abandon their obligations and those who are negligent of the rights of the creation, no matter how pious and obedient of the Sunnah they may be.

Over time, such gatherings transform and new concepts and ideas are introduced. In the initial period there were just gatherings of

speech) [*Bukhārī* [no.5146*]. They speak with our tongue. And had they spoken with a foreign language or the language of the Persians, there would not have been inclination towards them. However, the problem is that when they speak with eloquent speech/good style of speech, the people are lured towards them. This is from the height of fitnah.* [al-Fawzān, *Sharḥ Hadīthi Inna Kunnā Fī jāhilīyyatan* [pp.35-36]. The sayings of the Salaf are many in avoiding and not associating with the people of *bid^cah* and such gatherings. **[A]** al-Fuḍail bin Ā^cyyāḍ said, *"I met the best of people, all of them people of the Sunnah and they used to forbid from accompanying the people of innovation."* [al-Lālikā^cī, *Sharḥ Usūl al-Ei^ctiqād* [no.267]. **[B]** al-Ḥasan al-Baṣrī said, *"Do not sit with the people of innovation and desires, nor argue with them, nor listen to them."* [al-Dārimī, *as-Sunan* [1:121] **[C]** Ibrāhīm bin Maisarah said, *"Whoever honours an innovator has aided in the destruction of Islām."* [al-Lālikā^cī, *Sharḥ Usūl al-Ei^ctiqād* [1:139 no.267]. **[D]** Sufyān al-Thawrī said, *"Whoever listens to an innovator has left the protection of Allāh and is entrusted with the innovation."* [Abu Nu^caym, *al-Ḥilyah* [7:26], Ibn Baṭṭah [no.444]. **[E].** al-Shāf^cī said, *"That a person meets Allāh with every sin except shirk is better than meeting Him upon any one of the innovated beliefs."* [al-Baihaqī, *al-Ei^ctiqād* [p.158].

49 Also the new innovative phenomena of processions and demonstrations etc. that can be seen most recently by the Sūfis in Britain and elsewhere.

50 It is permissible to backbite and warn against the innovators who openly call and propagate their innovations. [Ibn Ḥajr, *Fatḥ al-Bārī* [7:86, 10:471], Nawawī, *Sharḥ Ṣaḥīḥ Muslim* [16:142], Ṣāleḥ ibn Sa^cd al-Suḥaimī, *Tanbīyyah Ulil al-Abṣār Ila Kamāl al-Dīn Wa Ma Fī al-Bid^cah Min Akhṭār* [p.189].

Milād,[51] some speeches, venerating poems and cooking fine food. Then the recitation of the Mawlid began, thereafter processions and demonstrations were orchestrated, which escalated in Muslim countries after a few years, when this was not the case in many of the Muslim countries.[52]

You will also find most of these customary practices and innovations occur in the big cities and not in the smaller towns or villages. These differences are accentuated in the different countries in different forms and means and in different languages. Sometimes these practices and innovations vary from country to country and from place to place. So this is a sign that these innovations change from place to place and adopt different shapes and forms[53] depending in the

---

[51] Cf. These Milādi shamans and whirling dervishes [Maḥmūd Aḥmad Mirpūrī, *Talkh Wa Shīrī* [pp.193-196, 202-206, 281-285]

[52] In a series of articles to be published we have presented research that the origins of the Mawlid are pre Islamic Pagan Turkic rituals and customary practices and Jalāl al-Dīn Rūmī (d.1273/671) the Sūfī who was the patron of the Sūfī Melviyyah (Mawlāwī) order and the chief proponent of the innovative practice of the 'whirling dervishes,' he was instrumental pushing the Mawlid we observe today. The Shī'te leaders and the Fātimids also played a significant role in propagating the *bidᶜah* of *Mawlid*. Neşet Çağatay in her paper asserts the Shīᶜa leaders of the Fatimids had such Mawlids recited for the Messenger of Allāh (ﷺ) and ᶜAlī (ؓ), this is precisely the Mawlid and Milād celebrations we have today. The Shīᶜa also have their own ideas and concepts of Milād, which they celebrate, in fact there is not much difference between how the Barailwī's, Sūfī's and Shīᶜa celebrate the Milād, two faces of the same coin. [Cf. Neşet Çağatay, *The Tradition of Mavlid Recitations in Islam Particularly in Turkey*, [pp.127+] Studia Islamic No. 28, 1968ce, Maisonneuve & Larose], Cf. Denis Mete's Ph.D paper *'Warest du nicht...' Presung des Propheten Muḥammad in Mevlūd-i-Keşfi'* [Wein University, 2013]

[53] **A Tremendous Benefit;** al-Barbahārī said, *"Beware of small innovations, because they will grow until they become large. This was the case with every innovation introduced into this Ummah. It began as something small, bearing resemblance to the truth, which is why those who entered into it were misled and then were unable to leave it. So it grew and became the religion that they followed, and thus deviated from the Straight Path and left Islām, and may Allāh have mercy upon you! Examine carefully the speech of everyone you hear from in your time particularly. So do not act in haste, and do not enter into anything from it until you ask and see: Did any of the Companions of the Messenger of Allāh (ﷺ) speak about it, or any of the Scholars? So if you find a narration from them about it, cling to it, do not go beyond it for anything and do not give precedence to anything over it and thus fall into the Fire."*

area you are in which all elucidate that they are things not from the prophetic way and nor are they recommended and nor do we find any evidence that the companions or Tābiᶜīn practised this.

The Dangers of Innovation

From the reprimand and censure that has been cited with regards to innovations then one of the reasons for this is to preserve the Dīn from becoming something that anyone can add or delete from. This is also to stop the people who think they can add any custom or practices and thereby making them a part of the Dīn, which would lead them to say, "What is the harm in doing so and so or "It is not a bad thing..." The main issue is that if people had a choice of adding anything into the

[al-Barbahārī, *Sharḥ as-Sunnah* [no.7-8]. **A Great Benefit;** by al-Fawzān, he said, *"Do not be lenient in anything from bidᶜah because it will increase and other things will be added to it which illustrates the dangers of bidᶜah, because if the door of bidᶜah is opened bidᶜah will increase. Do not be lenient with bidᶜah to the extent that it is said 'this is a small bidᶜah that does not harm.' bidᶜah is like a simmering coal, even though it is small in size it will increase in size/strength until it eventually burns the house or the shop or the entire locality. Most fires are from small sparks. Therefore, bidᶜah is not to be taken lightly rather the door to it is to be closed permanently. Indeed, the Messenger of Allāh (ﷺ) said, 'And beware of innovated matters [in the Dīn]'. This phrase used by the Messenger of Allāh (ﷺ) is a warning from bidᶜah in the absolute [unrestricted] sense, whether it is a small or large bidᶜah. The Messenger of Allāh (ﷺ) did not make exceptions for any types of bidᶜah whatsoever. The prohibition in this is ḥadīth is general regarding every type of bidᶜah. The Messenger of Allāh (ﷺ) also said 'the most evil of matters are the newly invented matters [in the Dīn]."* [al-Fawzān, *Ittiḥāf al-Qārī Bit Taᶜliqāt ᶜAla Sharḥ as-Sunnah lil Barbahārī* [p.60]

Dīn[54] it would become a joke and they could add or delete anything according to their desires.[55]

Another danger with innovations is that it makes you think the Messenger of Allāh (ﷺ) and his companions failed to perform certain good deeds, or they forgot to do them or they deliberately hid them from us.[56] We seek refuge with Allāh from such seriously inconceivable thoughts. If we think there is any capacity to formulate new righteous actions in later times, then why was the following āyah revealed.

[54] According to the various categorisations of *bidᶜah* one is ***Bidᶜah Fiᶜlī*** and ***Bidᶜah Tarkī***. ***Fiᶜlī*** is introducing something into the Dīn which resembles something already established in the *Sharīᶜah* with the intent and aim to increase in the worship of Allāh, there are some intricate differences between this and ***Bidᶜah Iḍāfiyyah*** [al-Shāṭibī, *al-Eiᶜtisām* [1:50-56]. For example the addition of an extra rakᶜah in the prayer or presenting an aspect of worship in a specific way opposing the method of the Messenger of Allāh (ﷺ). [Cf. al-Shāṭibī, *al-Eiᶜtisām* [1:367-445], Saᶜīd al-Ghamidī, *Ḥaqīqah al-Bidᶜah Wa Aḥkāmuhā* [2:35], ᶜAdawī, *Uṣūl Fi'l Bidᶜah Waʾl Sunan* [p.70]. Ṣāleḥ ibn Saᶜd al-Suḥaimī, *Tanbīyyah Ulil al-Abṣār Ila Kamāl al-Dīn Wa Ma Fī al-Bidᶜah Min Akhṭār* [p.99], al-Fawzān, *Kitāb al-Tawḥīd* [p.82], ᶜAlī bin Ḥasan al-Ḥalabī al-Atharī, *ᶜIlm al-Uṣūl al-Bidᶜah* [p.107]

[55] One of the consequences of innovations is that that innovators will have black faces on the Day of Judgement. ᶜAbd Allāh ibn ᶜAbbās (ﷺ) said in explanation of the āyah, ***"On the Day [some] faces will turn white and [some] faces will turn black." [Sūrah Āal-ᶜImrān:106],*** *"The faces of Ahl as-Sunnah will be white and the faces of the people of innovation and dissension will be black."* [Ibn Kathīr, *Tafsīr Ibn Kathīr*, [1:369], Ibn Jarīr, *Jāmᶜe Bayān ʾAn Tā'wīl Āay al-Qurʾān* [7:93], Ibn Qayyīm, *Ijtimāᶜ al-Juyūsh al-Islāmīyyah ᶜAla Ghazwa al-Muᶜaṭṭilah waʾl Jaḥmīyyah* [2:39]. al-Shāṭibī adds, an innovator follows his desires, openly rebels and opposes the Sharīᶜah and thus considers himself to be at the level of the legislator [*al-Eiᶜtisām* [1:61-70]

[56] This accusation they make against the Messenger of Allāh (ﷺ) is an abhorent one. Indeed, he was sent as a mercy for mankind and not one who would behave treacherously in letting the people know what had been revealed to him. Do these people not see that the Qurʾān says: **"Verily, those who conceal the clear proofs, evidences and the guidance, which We have sent down, after We have made it clear for the people in the Book, they are the ones cursed by Allāh and cursed by the cursers," [Baqarah:159].** So if something was revealed as part of the Dīn do they claim that the Messenger of Allāh (ﷺ) hid it in which case let them read this āyah? Or do they say he forgot? Either way, they have lied upon Allāh and his Messenger.

ٱلْيَوْمَ أَكْمَلْتُ لَكُمْ دِينَكُمْ

"This day I have perfected..." (Sūrah al-Ma'idah:3)[57]

After this command and completion of the Dīn there is no scope to innovate into it whether it is called *Ḥasanah* or anything else for that matter.[58] Another danger of innovations is that the people who innovate, in argument present new practices in a glamorous and alluring way, they cite the great rewards and benefits for such innovations beautifying[59] them so that the simple Muslims becomes caught up in the polemics.

[57] ᶜAbdul Azīz ibn ᶜAbd Allāh ibn Bāz said, *"This āyah decisively indicates that the Almighty Allâh has completed the religion for this Ummah, and has showered His blessings on them. His Messenger of Allāh (ﷺ) passed away only after he had imparted the complete Message of Allāh to the Ummah as well as his legislations concerning sayings and deeds. He also stressed that all things invented by people and then attributed to the religion of Islām are innovations and to be rejected, even if their inventors did so in good faith. It is established that the Companions of the Messenger of Allāh (ﷺ) and the righteous Successors after them warned the people against innovations as they add to Islām and legislate what is not permitted by Allāh, in line with the enemies of Allāh such as the Jews and the Christians who added to their religion and innovated what was not allowed by Allāh. Moreover, to admit innovation in Islām is to admit that Islām is incomplete and imperfect. Such a belief is not only an evil but contradicts the following āyah: "This day have I perfected your religion for you," and the sayings of the Messenger of Allāh (ﷺ) which warn us against innovations."* [ᶜAbdul ᶜAzīz ibn ᶜAbd Allāh ibn Bāz, *Wūjūb Lazūm al-Sunnah Waʾl Ḥazr Minaʾ Bidᶜah* [pp.6-7]. This āyah is further explained by the Ḥadīth of ᶜAbd Allāh ibn ᶜAmr al-ᶜĀs (ﷺ) who said the Messenger of Allāh (ﷺ) said as part of a longer Ḥadīth, *"It was the duty of every Prophet that came before me to guide his followers to what he knew was good for them and warn them against what he knew was bad for them..."* [*Muslim* [no.1844].

[58] Imām Mālik said, *"Whoever thinks there is such a thing as good innovation in Islām, has accused the Messenger of Allāh (ﷺ) of treachery because Allāh said,* ***"This day I have perfected your religion...,"*** *so what was not religion then, is not religion today."* [al-Shaṭibī, *al-Eiᶜtisām* [1:38]

[59] It is from amongst the traps of Shayṭān that he beautifies sin and evil, in this instance *bidᶜah*, to people. One can see in the Qurʾān that he beautified and allured Ādam towards eating from the forbidden tree by saying: **"Then Shayṭān (Satan) whispered to him, saying: "O Adam! Shall I lead you to the Tree of Eternity and to a kingdom that will never waste away?" [Ṭā-hā:120].** And to the people of Makkah in their opposition to the Messenger of Allāh (ﷺ) **"And (remember) when Shayṭān**

This is not a mere claim, if you look at the Muslims today you will find them abandoning the obligatory actions which have been obligated by Allāh, like praying[60] and fasting but at the same instance they are involved in practising all kinds of innovations and customary practices. They believe, by abandoning such innovations they will be deprived of the great rewards and hence will be questioned by Allāh. This is such a loss in that the obligatory acts are not being practised and they are engrossed themselves in innovations and customary practices.

Another major danger and problem with innovations as mentioned by the pious predecessors *(Salaf al-Sālihīn)* is that the innovator or the one who practices innovations is unlikely to repent from them.[61] A sinner is often aware of the evil effect of his sin and so the likelihood of him repenting and returning to righteousness is very high. An innovator does not think he is doing anything wrong in any instance[62],

(Satan) made their (evil) deeds seem fair to them and said, "No one of mankind can overcome you this Day (of the battle of Badr) and verily, I am your neighbour (for each and every help)." But when the two forces came in sight of each other, he ran away and said "Verily, I have nothing to do with you. Verily! I see what you see not. Verily! I fear Allāh for Allāh is Severe in punishment." [Anfāl:48]. May All protect us from the plots of the Shayṭān. Āmīn.

60 However, Aḥmed Raḍha Barailwī records that *"Satan prays Ṣalāh and when he was asked why he was doing this, he said I am repenting to Allāh"* [Ahmed Raḍha Khān, *Malfūẓāt* [1:12]. This is undoubtedly a baseless story amongst his many fables.

61 Anas bin Mālik (ﷺ) narrates that the Messenger of Allāh (ﷺ) said, *"Allāh has closed the door of repentance on all those who are innovators."* [Ṭabarāni, *Mu^{c}jam al-Awsaṭ* [8:62 no.4713] from *Majma^{c}a al-Baḥrain Fī Zawā$^{\circ}$id al-Mu^{c}ajamain*]. Haithamī said, *"Its narrators are of Ṣaḥīḥ al-Bukhārī except Harūn bin Mūsa Farwī but he is also trustworthy."* [Haithamī, *Majma^{c}a al-Zawā$^{\circ}$id* [10:189]. al-Albānī also authenticated it and cites its various routes. [al-Albānī, *Silsilah Aḥadīth al-Ṣahīḥah* [4:154 no.1620]. It was authenticated as 'Ḥasan' by Mundhirī in *at-Targhīb* [1:86]. The innovator becomes so deluded with his own self that he thinks what he is upon is the Sunnah yet is no more than that which leads him astray destroying any deeds he thinks he is accumulating. Allāh says **"Say (O Muhammad (ﷺ): "Shall We tell you the greatest losers in respect of (their) deeds? "Those whose efforts have been wasted in this life while they thought that they were acquiring good by their deeds!" [al-Kahf:102-104].**

62 Shawkānī said, *"Sunnah is not established by mere practice or experience, an individual doing a bid^{c}ah with the intention and belief it is a Sunnah does not exclude*

on the contrary, he thinks he is doing something praiseworthy and rewarding which may lead him to salvation.[63] How will such an individual return to the truth and repent when he believes he is doing something good and rewarding?[64]

Answering the Confusion[65] of *Ahl al-Bid^c^ah*

So far, we have mentioned some of the fundamental and important points as they relate to innovations in a general manner. We now wish to address and clarify some of the doubts and confusion the Muslims fall into. Some people have vehemently and staunchly clung onto *Bid^c^ah Ḥasanah* and promoted it to such an extent that it has led to the emergence of a new group[66] who abandon the obligatory and

or expel himself from the rulling of being an innovator." [Shawkānī, *Tuḥfa al-Zākirīn* [p.140].

63 This is why Ibn Qayyim said, *"One should know that an innovation is more dangerous than light sin."* [Ibn Qayyim, *Madārij al-Sālikīn* [1:222]

64 This is the reason why Sufyān al-Thawrī said, *"Iblīs favours innovations more in comparison to sins because one can repent from sins but he does not repent from his innovations."* [al-Baghawī, *Sharḥ al-Sunnah* [1:216]

65 Ponder on the words of Allāh about those who invent new affairs into the religion such as calling upon other than him! Indeed, the people of innovation and *shirk* have no evidence but that which can be destroyed with the slightest force. **"The parable of those who take protectors other than Allāh is that of the spider, who builds (to itself) a house; but truly the flimsiest of houses is the spider's house; - if they but knew." [al-^c^Ankabūt:41].**

66 These groups are many. Seeing as the author was from the sub-continent it is not difficult to see that at the head of these groups are the 'Barailwī Sūfīs' who advocate all types of *shirk* and *bid^c^ah* as a foundation of their sect and who claim to be staunch Ḥanafī's but yet their ways are far removed from Abū Ḥanīfah. There founding father was Aḥmed Raḍha Khān [d.1921] in India. His belief was in opposition to the Salaf in almost all aspects of Tawḥīd and Sunnah and is far too great to mention here and his many works are a testament to this. Furthermore, the sayings recorded from him are baseless stories, which are nothing short of blasphemy. One such incident is what he said his saint *"Sayyīdī Mūsā Suhāg (Note; he was a Male) Rehmatullah alayhi looked towards the heavens and whilst addressing Allāh as 'husband' he said "Send the Mīan (ie send the husband-this is referring to Mian being Allāh) or take your bride."* [*Malfūẓāt* [2:240]. Another such saying from him is that he said his creed was

mandatory commands and the rights of Allāh and yet have a strong fervent desire[67] and extreme longing for innovations and new practices.

In this day and age numerous customs and practices which have no basis from the Messenger of Allāh (ﷺ) or the companions have added to the Dīn. From them are the annual celebrations of the saints ie the *urs*, making food and offering it as reward on behalf of the deceased on the 3rd day, 10th day, the 20th and the 40th, offering sacrifices,[68] reciting Fātiḥah,[69] doing *Tawāf* of graves, lighting candles on graves[70] and washing graves.[71] There are numerous other such innovations and

that *"The prophet is alive in his grave as he was in the worldly life so much so that his wives are presented to him so he can be intimate with them."* [Aḥmed Raḍha Khān, *Malfūẓāt* [3:204]. May Allāh protect us from misguidance. Cf. to Eḥsān Ilāhī Ẓahīr's *'al-Barailwīyyah'* for a detailed expose. **An Extra Benefit;** It is incumbent to stay away from such a sect. Qāḍī Abū Yaᶜlā said, *"There is ijmāᶜ (consensus) from the Companions and the Tābi'īn as regards disassociating and cutting-off from the innovators."* [Qāḍī Abū Yaᶜlā, *Ḥajr al-Mubtadī'* [p.32].

67 Shāh Muḥammad Ismāᶜīl, the illustrious author of the monumental work, Taqwiyah al-Imān said, *"Most of preferred opinions of the later jurists and Sūfīs which are based on mere ambiguity and in order to seek some religious benefits are done without any legislated evidences from the sharīᶜah. They formulate new affairs in aspects of worship and dealings and at times self interpret Uṣūls (principles) in the Dīn making them specific and thereby formulating new Uṣūls. They do this in order to spread new customs which were non existent in the times before. Likewise, other such customs ie the Maᶜkūs Ṣalāh and making taqlīd of one specific Imām obligatory or transferring the deeds of the living people to the souls of the deceased...."* [Shāh Muḥammad Ismāᶜīl, *Ayḍāḥ al-Ḥaq al-Ṣarīḥ Fī Aḥkām al-Mayyat Waᵓl Ḍharīḥ* [p.81]

68 Cf. The legal status of sacrificing and vowing in the name of other Allāh [Maḥmūd Aḥmad Mirpūrī, *Fatāwa Ṣirāt al-Mustaqīm* [pp.39-41].

69 Cf. The custom of reciting Fātiḥah for the deceased is a *bidᶜah* [Maḥmūd Aḥmad Mirpūrī, *Fatāwa Ṣirāt al-Mustaqīm* [pp.273-287].

70 Refer to reference in the previous footnote.

71 These are just some of the corrupt practices advocated by Aḥmed Raḍha. It is a shame that many other Ḥanafī's from the Deobandī and Jamāᶜah al-Tablīgh sect have become influenced by the Barailwī's in their creed and fiqh. Refer to the book of Shaikh Ṭālib ur-Rehmān's *'al-Deobandīyyah,' 'Jamāt ut-Tablīgh'* and *'The Aqidah of the Barailwi's and Deobandi's'* [Cf. http://www.salafiri.com/the-aqidah-of-the-barailwis-and-deobandis-shaikh-talib-ur-rehman/] and *'The Deobandis & The British Government.'* http://www.salafiri.com/the-deobandis-the-british-government/ and much more at www.salafiri.com] in which it is clear that the creed of these sects especially in relation to aspects of Tawḥīd al-Ulūhiyyah and al-Asmā Waᵓl Ṣifāt they

customary practices, which have no basis in the first three blessed generations of Islām. However, before we discuss the impermissibility of the aforementioned practices it is important to address some of the doubts and misconceptions that are presented by the people of innovation.

The First Doubt - New Affairs

They say if everything new is considered to be innovations, then what about things like aeroplanes, cars, glasses and other such new inventions in our times,[72] they are also innovations, hence why are they used?

all resemble each other. Some examples include, they are all Ashᶜarī, Māturidī and at times Jahmī by way of taᶜtīl, ta'wīl, and tafwīḍ of the attributes of Allāh. [cf. *al-Muhannad ᶜAla Mufannad*]. They all agree that Imān does not increase or decrease and actions are not a part of Imān thus being from the Murjīᶜah and it is for this reason ᶜAbdul Qādir Jīlānī placed them amongst the 72 deviated sects in his *Ghunīyah ut-Tālibīn* [p.252]. ᶜAlī Nāṣir al-Faqīhi said, *"From the aforementioned sects are the Kullābīyyah, Ashaᶜirah, Murji'ah and every sect which has adopted the way of ta'wīl in the Names and Ṣifāt of Allāh. They have subjected the texts to their intellects and whatever it comprehends they accept and whatever it does not, they reject. Whereas the intellect is not the criterion to understand the texts of the Sharīᶜah because the intellects differ."* [ᶜAlī Nāṣir al-Faqīhi, *al-Bidᶜah Ḍawābiṭha Wa Atharuhā al-Sayyᶜia Fiᶜl Ummah* [p.27]

[72] Then it can be said that these new technologies are from that which has nothing to do with worship and nor are they intended for reward or to seek closeness to Allāh in order to please him but from the affairs of the Dunyā. These things can be seen as 'mubāh' (permitted see below), then these are merely matters which are permitted in the Sharīᶜah (shaking hands, eating food, wearing clothes) [and are not from the affairs of worship] but they are being performed in a new way (i.e. with something of excess compared to previously). This has nothing to do with matters of worship (ᶜIbādah) which the Innovators try to justify, which are opposed to the Sunnah in either their foundation, or their details. [al-Shāṭibī, *al-Eiᶜtisām* [1:319]. No one from amongst the Ummah [even those who are the Sūfī's] have ever said that to use such technology is from amongst the Dīn and hence a *bidᶜah* which leads astray as everything in the affairs of the Dunyā is permissible unless there is a text from the Dīn to restrict or forbid it. How ironic is it that the modern Barailwī's use the actions of *Dunyā* [driving cars] and try to justify their *bidᶜah* in the Dīn yet their founders played a different game. Let us present a gift to the Barailwīs to show that in application even their

Answer

On the apparent this seems like a very crucial and important point, but the individual who knows the correct definition of *bid^cah* will not fall into this error. The only people who present this doubt are those who are unfamiliar with the definition of *bid^cah* or those who want to deliberately confuse and deceive the people. We have clarified in the beginning that innovations are practices that are formulated in the Dīn with the intention of seeking reward and benefits. The words of the Messenger of Allāh (ﷺ) are clear, *"Whosoever introduces something new in "...**our affair...**"*[73] this does not mention worldly things.

There is no one in this world who travels on aeroplanes and thinks it is rewarding or believes that wearing glasses is rewarding and a means of salvation. likewise, and similarly no one believes using a telephone or radio will incur more reward or benefits. Furthermore, using new inventions cannot be understood to be innovations because they will not change the Dīn when they are acted upon. Thus, this is why they cannot be called innovations and nor do they become a part

founder Aḥmed Raḍha Khān held that *bid^cah* in the Dunyā was distinct from the reprehensible one in the Dīn. Aḥmed Raḍha Khān said whilst giving the ruling that tobacco is 'Mubāh' and 'Ḥalāl' that *"Then it being a bid^cah is not a blameworthy issue as it is a bid^cah from the issues of eating and drinking [Dunyā] and not a bid^cah in the Dīn. Therefore, to establish it [tobacco] as Ḥarām will be a difficult task for those who seek to do so."* [Aḥmed Raḍha Khān, *Risālah Hukka Tul Marjān Lahūm Hukum ad-Dukhān* [p.3] cf. Aḥmed Raḍha Khān's *Fatāwa Riḍhwīyyah* [11:41] and *Aḥkām Sharī^cyyat* [Part 3 no: 37]

[73] Muḥammad Ra^ɔīs Nadwī said, *"We find from this Prophetic ḥadīth that every statement, action and method that has become customary amongst the Muslims are futile and rejected in opposition to the texts. Furthermore, all the companions in general abandoned taqlīd and the leader of the Barailwī sect, Aḥmad Yār Khān Nu^caimī has also acknowledged this.(Jā^ɔ al-Ḥaq, printed in Jāmnūr Delhī, 1361H [1:27] and thus the ardent muqallids oppose the way of the Messenger of Allāh (ﷺ) and the way of the companions. This Prophetic Ḥadīth mentions the solution to protect oneself from the sheer differences that are to arise amongst the Ummah. Thus it is obligatory to hold onto the Prophetic Sunnah and the Sunnah of the rightly guided Khulāfa and to abstain from inventing new affairs without rendering them to be a part of the Dīn as they are innovations and misguidance..."* [Muḥammad Ra^ɔīs Nadwi, *Ḍhamīr Ka Buḥrān* [p.238]

of the Dīn. Whereas as the customary innovations that are practised with the intention of seeking reward, not only have they become part of the Dīn but rather they are understood to be more mandatory and more important than the obligatory acts.

Similarly, we have the issues of clothes, no one wears specific clothes and then thinks that they will receive more reward and nor did the Messenger of Allāh (ﷺ) place any restrictions on clothing except that they must cover the body appropriately. During the life of the Messenger of Allāh (ﷺ) the companions would wear what the Messenger of Allāh (ﷺ) would wear. The same applies to what the Messenger of Allāh (ﷺ) would eat. He disliked certain foods but the companions would happily eat them. Therefore, associating these things with the Dīn has no correlation[74] or whether they are rewarding or incur sin. An innovation is something that is formulated with the intention of seeking reward but no evidence or example can be found from the Messenger of Allāh (ﷺ) or the companions.

The Second Doubt - *Ijtihād* or Innovations

Some people confuse ijtihād and innovations thereby causing confusion by saying that ijtihad is also something new in the Dīn so why is that not an innovation

Answer

There is no connection between *ijtihād* and innovations. The need for ijtihād arises when a new situation or issue takes place and a mujtahid

[74] In reality these issues of the Dunyā fall under that which is *'Mubāh' [permissible].* The people of Uṣūl [jurisprudence] have defined this as *"Something which if performed there is no reward attached to it and if left no sin is attached to it."* Then we have specifically given this definition as it is from the Ḥanafī books of Uṣūl so that they may ponder over it. This is what has been mentioned in *Tawḍhīh* [p.26], *Khulāsah al-Afkār* [p.159], *Fatāwa al-Shāmī* [1:123 and 1:653], *Uṣūl Sarkhasī* [1:112]. So why is that then the Barailwī's will go against what their own books have recorded?

uses the Qur'ān and Ḥadīth and the actions of the companions to issue a ruling. Therefore, the basis of ijtihād is the Qur'ān and Ḥadīth.[75] The Āyāt and the aḥadīth that are used as evidence are conclusive and evidences in themselves. Whereas, innovations are spread without evidence and neither is there a need for them. The excuses they put forth in their defence for these innovations were also prevalent during the era of the Messenger of Allāh (ﷺ) and the companions. For example, what is the need to place objects on graves, offer sacrifices or celebrate the birthdays of saints?

Similarly, we know graves existed during the time of the Messenger of Allāh (ﷺ) and the rightly guided Khalīfs. Furthermore, some of these graves were of the best people of this Ummah.[76] During their times they also had opportunities to offer sacrifices and place ornamented garments over the graves, despite this they did not feel the

[75] Ijtihād means to strive for something in the Dīn and in this instance it would mean to exert effort to reach a verdict based on the texts of the Dīn [*Qāmūs al-Waḥīdi* [p.34]. Whereas, *bid^cah* is far removed from Ijtihād and is seen as inventing something into the Dīn which has no basis in it and this is rejected as per the ḥadīth of Ā^cishah (رضي الله عنها) *"Whoever introduced something new in our affair, which was not from it, will have it rejected."* So Ijtihād is not introduction of a new thing in the 'affair [Dīn]' but is based upon it due to a new need arising to give a contemporary verdict. One can refer to Badī^c al-Dīn's Shāh al-Rāshidī al-Sindhī's book *'Tanqīd Sadīd Bi'l Risālah Ijtihād wa'l Taqlīd'* for a juristical viewpoint on Ijtihād and how at times it has been abused by the blind followers of the madhabs.

[76] The graves of the Ṣahābah existed at the time of the Messenger of Allāh (ﷺ) and today and there are a plethora of verses and narrations concerning the status of the Ṣahābah and the first three generations. Suffice it to mention one. The Messenger of Allāh (ﷺ) said, *"There will come upon the people a time when a group from amongst the people will go off to fight and it will be said to them: Is there any amongst you who has seen the Messenger of Allāh (ﷺ)? So they will say: Yes. So victory will be granted to them. So a group will go off to fight and it will be said to them: Is there any amongst you who were the Companions of the Messenger of Allāh (ﷺ)? So they will say: Yes. So victory will be granted to them. Then a group will go off to fight and it will be said to them: Is there any amongst you who have seen the companions of the Companions of the Messenger of (ﷺ)? So they will say: Yes. So victory will be granted to them."* [*Bukhārī* [no.3649] and *Muslim* [no.3456] from Abū Sa^cīd al-Khudrī (رضي الله عنه)]. So not only were the Ṣahābah blessed but the very era they lived in became blessed due to them being within it upholding the Dīn. Yet we find them being the most severe in safeguarding the Dīn from *bid^cah* and alteration! May Allāh be pleased with them all.

need to do such actions and there was also nothing that prevented them such actions therefore, how can we make these excuses now?

Furthermore, there is unanimous agreement on the need for ijtihād by the scholars and no one has denied or refuted this. Whereas innovations are rampant in our times as such they were not even practised by one of the four Imāms or any faqih of the *madhabs* nor did they issue any verdicts to practise them. When the people started to habitually abandon obligatory acts as well as the Sunnah, the spirit of Islām began to diminish. Then some evil scholars,[77] leaders and free willed rulers introduced such customs in to the Dīn by which they harmed Islām and also achieved their worldly benefits and the common people would think they have achieved and fulfilled a major obligation of the Dīn.

The Third Doubt - But What is the Harm?

Another universal common doubt, which is presented by the innovators is, what is the harm in doing certain actions. This doubt is also global and sometimes good Sunnis also become embroiled and fall into this trap. They become confused and get engrossed in this intellectual difficulty. They claim they practise righteous actions which are virtuous deeds and therefore what is the harm in practising them. Although they acknowledge such actions were established by the Messenger of Allāh (ﷺ) or the companions, there is no harm in them so why do you warn against them?

Answer[78]

Performing righteous actions is always commendable and praiseworthy. Also those who prohibit the practising of established

[77] The Shaikh has answered a specific question in this regard titled, evil scholars and innovations under the chapter heading, *'The various forms of innovations'*[Maḥmūd Aḥmad Mirpūrī, *Fatāwa Ṣirāt al-Mustaqīm* [pp.435-437]

[78] Refer to footnote above about ***Bidᶜah Iḍāfiyyah***, under the heading of the definition of *bidᶜah*.

righteous actions are also sinful. However, the question essentially is what are righteous actions or good deeds. Who will define what a righteous action or good deed is? Or who will conclude it is correct, rewardable and beneficial or on the contrary if the deed is bad, evil and sinful? Furthermore, who will derive the method of performing these righteous actions? If every individual was to establish and formulate their own way of performing righteous deeds and their own way of defining what a righteous action is then the Dīn would become a mockery and it would also invalidate the reason why the Prophets were sent.

Only the Messenger of Allāh (ﷺ) can define and clarify what righteous deeds are. Every individual does not have the right to define what a righteous action is and then perform them in a particular manner. Numerous incidences occurred during the time of the companions where they performed righteous deeds thinking they were virtuous because Allāh was worshipped and praised but despite this they were prohibited.

When they were informed this was not the way of the Messenger of Allāh (ﷺ) they stopped immediately. We shall present some examples of this very shortly, examples of virtuous actions that appeared to be good and there was no harm in performing them but the companions prevented them from becoming prevalent only because they were not established from the Messenger of Allāh (ﷺ).

The First Evidence
The Hadith of the Pebbles

ᶜAbd Allāh ibn Masᶜūd (رضي الله عنه) narrates the Ḥadīth of the pebbles,[79]

[79] It is highly recommended that the reader refer to and study the very beneficial book by Muḥammad bin Ramaḍhān al-Ḥājirī called *'Hadyas Ṣahābah Fī Mu'āmalāt Ahlil Bidᶜah Fawāid Min Ḥadīth ᶜAbd Allāh Ibn Masᶜūd Wa Ashāb ul-Ḥalaq.'* This book will give the reader an insight into the excuses used by *Ahl al-Bidᶜah* and the Salafs response to them. Ubaid al-Jābirī also has a book in explanation of this narration, thus, the avid reader reader is advised to refer to them. Narrated from al-Ḥakam ibn al-Mubārak who narrates from ᶜAmr ibn Salima al-Ḥamdāni, *"We used to sit by the door*

"[c]Abd Allāh ibn Mas[c]ūd heard some people one day raising their voices and reciting La Ilaha IllalAllāh and sending salutations on the Messenger of Allāh (ﷺ) in the Masjid. He went to them and said, "We did not learn this method of making zikr from the Messenger of Allāh (ﷺ) hence you

of [c]Abd Allāh ibn Mas[c]ūd before the Morning Prayer, so that when he came out we would walk with him to the mosque. (One day) Abū Mūsā al-Ash[c]arī came to us and said: "Has Abū [c]Abdal-Rahmān come out yet?" We replied No. So he sat down with us until he came out. When he came out, we all stood along with him, so Abu Musa said to him: "O Abū [c]Abdal-Rahmān! I have just seen something in the mosque which I considered wrong, but all praise is for Allāh, I did not see anything except good in it." He inquired: "What is it?" Abū Mūsā replied: "If you live you will see it. I saw in the mosque people sitting in circles awaiting the Prayer. In each circle they had pebbles in their hands and a man would say: Repeat Allāhu Akbar a hundred times. So they would repeat it a hundred times. Then he would say: say la ilāha illAllāh a hundred times. So they would say it a hundred times. Then he would say: say subhanAllāh a hundred times. So they would say it a hundred times." Ibn Mas[c]ūd asked, "What did you say to them?" Abū Mūsā said. "I did not say anything to them. Instead I waited to hear your view on it." Ibn Mas[c]ūd replied: "Would that you had ordered them to count their evil deeds and assured them that their good deeds would not be lost!" Then we went along with him until he came to one of these circles whereby he stood and said: "What is this I see you doing?" They replied: "O Abū [c]Abdal-Rahmān! These are pebbles upon which we are counting takbir, taḥlil and tasbiḥ." He said: "Count your evil deeds instead. I assure you that none of your good deeds will be lost. Woe to you, O Ummah of Muḥammad (ﷺ), how quickly you go to destruction! Here are your Prophet's Companions available in abundance (mutawafirun). And there are his clothes which have not yet decayed and his bowl which is unbroken. By Him in Whose Hand is my soul! Either you are following a Religion that is better guided than the Religion of Muḥammad (ﷺ) or you are opening a door of misguidance." They said: "O Abū [c]Abdal-Rahmān! By Allāh, we only intend good!" He said: "How many are there who intend good but do not achieve it. Indeed, Allāh's Messenger said to us: A people will recite the Qur'an but it will not pass beyond their throats. By Allāh! I do not know, but perhaps most of them are from among you." Then he left them. [c]Amr ibn Salima said: We saw most of those people fighting against us on the day of Nahrawān, on the side of the Khawārij." [al-Dārimī, *as-Sunan* [1:79] graded authentic by al-Haithamī, *al-Majma[c]a* [1:181, 189], al-Haithamī, *az-Zawājir* [no.51], al-Albānī, *as-Ṣaḥīḥah* [no.2005], *ar-Radd [c]Alal-Habashī*, [pp.45-47], [c]Abdul-Muḥsin al-[c]Abbād, *al-Hathth al-Ittibā as-Sunnah* [p.49], Bakr Abū Zaid, *Tas-hīh ud-Du[c]ā*, [pp.149, 153, 154], Hussaīn [c]Asad, *Sunan al-Dārimī* [no.210], Mashūr Ḥasan al-Salmān, *al-[c]Amr bil Ittibā* [pp.83-84].

are innovating. ᶜAbd Allāh ibn Masᶜūd did not stop repeating his point up until the people left the Masjid."[80]

This has been cited in the explanation of the famous book of Ḥanafī Fiqh *Durr al-Mukhtār* namely *Hāshīyyah Ṭawālᶜe* and in *Fatāwa Bazāzīyyah* as well as others. It has also been transmitted in *Sunan al-Dārimī* in detail, which we shall mention later.

We should be honest, sincere and think, was ᶜAbd Allāh ibn Masᶜūd (.) prohibiting these people from a sinful action? They were only making Zikr and sending salutations upon the Messenger of Allāh (.), was this impermissible? Could the people not have objected and said what the harm is in what we are doing is? If in this era such Zikr and chants are stopped which were not established from the Messenger of Allāh (.), there would be an uproar among the people who would go into a frenzy and uncontrollable chaotic commotion and sheepishly say (about us); "look they are stopping us from making Zikr of Allāh, they stop us from making dua, what is he harm, we are only remembering Allāh and praising him"?

In reality no Muslim prevents other Muslims from remembering Allāh, or from sending salutations upon the Messenger of Allāh (.). Is there anyone who has the audacity to reject these actions? The point is, what ᶜAbd Allāh ibn Masᶜūd (.) said to the people, that we do not consider this to be a virtuous action because it was not approved by the Messenger of Allāh (.). Furthermore, we can not attain the pleasure of Allāh except with the method the Messenger of Allāh (.) informed us and we will not accept anything less than this.

[80] Ibn Ḥajr al-Asqalānī said, *"The wording of zikr is tawqīfī (i.e. acts of worship which must be done as prescribed in the texts), and they have special characteristics that cannot be subject to analogy. So one must adhere to the wording as it was narrated.* [Ibn Ḥajr, *Fatḥ al-Bārī* [11:112]

The Second Evidence
Ḥadīth of the 2 rak^{c}ahs as optional prayer at the E^{c}īd Musallah.[81]

Can the Muftī of today say ^{c}Alī (ﷺ) declared a prayer to be unlawful, we seek refuge in Allāh from this.[82] Who has the audacity to issue a fatwa against ^{c}Alī (ﷺ) who vehemently shunned innovations. We ask the dear reader to have an open, sound and intelligent mind to decide what the real criterion is for righteous or evil actions and the necessity to abstain from innovations.[83]

[81] Cf. p.34 for details concerning praying optional prayer before the E^{c}id Ṣalāh. Another tremendous ḥadīth in this regard is reported from Anas (ﷺ) wherein 3 men came to the house of the wife of the Messenger of Allāh (ﷺ) and said that they would continuously fast, pray all night long and never marry. On hearing this the Messenger of Allāh (ﷺ) said *"Are you the people who said such things? I swear by Allāh that I fear Allāh more than you do, and I am most obedient and dutiful among you to Him, but still, I observe fasting (sometimes) and break it (at others); I perform (optional) prayer (at night sometimes) and sleep at night (at others); I also marry. So whoever turns away from my Sunnah (i.e., my way) is not from me."* [*al-Bukhārī* [no.5063], *Muslim* [no.1401]. There is the additional wording in Sunan Abū Dāwūd where the Messenger of Allāh (ﷺ) said to the three men *"Beware from what is bid^{c}ah, for verily Bida^{c}h is misguidance"*. [The chain is Ṣaḥīḥ according to al-Albānī, *Sunan Abū Dāwūd* [no.4611], al-Ḥākim, *al-Mustadrak* [4:508]. The benefits from this narration are far reaching and include the fact that none of these acts of praying, fasting etc. are seen as reprehensible but yet the: al-Kam (number), al-Kayf (form), al-Jins (type), al-Ṣabab (cause, reason), al-Makān (place) and al-Zamān (time) were all different to how the Messenger of Allāh (ﷺ) performed these acts of worship. Also the Messenger of Allāh (ﷺ) equated such actions [that have a basis in the Dīn but yet not stipulated specifically by him as something against his Sunnah hence his saying, *"So whoever turns away from my Sunnah (i.e., my way) is not from me."* Another Ḥadīth mentions as narrated by ^{c}Amr bin Shu^{c}aib (ﷺ) who said, *"The Messenger of Allāh (ﷺ) pronounced 12 takbīrs in the E^{c}īd prayer, seven (7) in the first rak^{c}ah and five (5) in the second rak^{c}ah and he did not pray anything before or after this."* [*Ibn Mājah* [no.1377]

[82] This discussion is referring to the statement of ^{c}Alī (ﷺ) which has preceded under the discussion of categories of *bid^{c}ah* p.34.

[83] The Shaikh has answered a specific question in his Fatāwa he says, *"Therefore, there is no doubt whatsoever that there is no prayer before or after the E^{c}īd prayer"...* he further says, *"and because the Messenger of Allāh (ﷺ) did not offer any prayer before or after the E^{c}īd prayer, it is better not to offer any optional or Sunnah prayers*

The Third Evidence
Saying *Alhamdulillāh Wassalāmu ʿAla Rasūlullāh* When Sneezing

The third Ḥadīth in this regard is from Sunan at-Tirmidhī in which Nāfʿe reports,

> "That a man sneezed by the side of Ibn ʿUmar (⚬) and said, "All praise is due to Allāh and peace and blessings be upon His Messenger!" So Ibn ʿUmar said: "And I say All praise is due to Allāh and peace and blessings be upon His Messenger, but this is not how the Messenger (⚬) taught us; rather he taught us to say 'All praise is due to Allāh in all situations."[84]

ʿAbd Allāh Ibn ʿUmar[85] (⚬) was so strong and firm on the Sunnah that anything opposing it was unacceptable to him. So was he opposed to sending salutations upon the The Messenger of Allāh (⚬)? In fact he was so firm on the Sunnah he was ready to sacrifice his life and this is the reason why he said "We will only say what our Prophet (⚬) taught us." So did not Ibn ʿUmar (⚬) warn against something virtuous (even though it was not established from the Messenger of Allāh (⚬))? Was there any harm in saying these words? The people say to us what is the harm in such and such thing but we say according to us this is

---

before the Eʿid prayer." (the Shaikh used the words 'better' referring to the action of those who pray the Tahhayatul Masjid [Is it permissible to pray optional prayers before the Eʿīd Ṣalāh [Maḥmūd Aḥmad Mirpūrī, *Fatāwa Ṣirāt al-Mustaqīm* [pp.310-311]

[84] *Ṣaḥīḥ Sunan Tirmidhī* [no.2738], Ḥakim, *al-Mustadrak* [4:265-266], al-Mizzī, *Tahdhīb al-Kamāl* [6:553]

[85] He is the illustrious companion ʿAbd Allāh ibn ʿUmar (⚬) the son of ʿUmar al-Fārūq (⚬). He was a prominent authority in hadīth and law, and was known for his piety, honesty and erudition in Prophetic traditions. He was too young to participate at Uhud, but participated at Khandaq and later battles. He is the narrator of hundreds of hadīth and was known for his being staunch in the love and following the Sunnah of the Messenger of Allāh (⚬) from a young age. He has 714 narrations in *Ṣaḥīḥ Bukhārī* and 586 in *Ṣaḥīḥ Muslim*. [Ibn Ḥajr, *al-Iṣābah* [4:182,183,184,185], Ibn Ḥibbān, *Thiqāt* [3:67], Bukhārī, *Tārīkh al-Kabīr* [5:189], Dhahabī, *Sīyar Aʿlām an-Nabulā* [3:203-241].

the biggest harm and problem in that it is not established from the Messenger of Allāh (ﷺ) because anything that opposes his way is the biggest harm and problem.

Two Example from the Books of Fiqh
The First Example

Baḥr ur-Rāʾiq[86] mentions,

> "It is prohibitively disliked to say, "Come to a good deed (ie *Hayya ᶜAla Khair al-ᶜAmal*) (in the *Ādhān* instead of *Hayya Alas Ṣalāh*) because this is not established from the Messenger of Allāh (ﷺ)." [al-Junnah Li-Ahl al-Sunnah][87]

So dear readers, these words do not appear to be bad but we cannot use them whenever we want. Likewise, we can not use words and phrases in our supplications, invocations, and salutations if they are not established from the Messenger of Allāh (ﷺ). For example, the Messenger of Allāh (ﷺ) recited lengthy supplications in the funeral prayers with great humility, however the people abandon these supplications and instead recite shorter fabricated supplications after the prayer. This is very odd and strange and it also opposes and contradicts the way of the Messenger of Allāh (ﷺ).

The Messenger of Allāh (ﷺ) advised us to visit the graves, give salutations to the deceased and pray for their forgiveness. We have abandoned this advice of the Messenger of Allāh (ﷺ) and rather we visit the relatives of the deceased. We openly smoke cigarettes and blow the fumes into the room and at the same time whilst having tea we recite *Sūrah al-Fātiḥah* and further organise gatherings for the Qurʾān to be recited. When the fact of the matter is, such people fail to understand why *Sūrah al-Fātiḥah* was revealed. Furthermore, no *madhab* has specified that one should make their supplication by

[86] Ibn Najīm, *Baḥr al-Rāʾiq Sharḥ Kunz ad-Daqāʾiq* [1:275], he cites this from a Shāfᶜī text.

[87] The author of this book is ᶜAbdul Ghanī Khān and the full name of the book is, *al-Junnah Li Aṣḥāb al-Sunnah.*

visiting the relatives of the deceased. We keep our supplications to ourselves for months on end and when we find some meagre time we visit the relatives and offer them our supplications!

Whereas the truth is that the relatives can only receive our condolences but not our supplications and we do all of this, not for the deceased but rather to keep face with their living relatives. This is evident by the sheer fact we visit the living relatives and offer our supplications just to show our attendance. We can label such practices as family customary practices or we can call them the customary norms of our countries but for Allāh sake do not have the bold audacity to attribute them and for them to be a part of Islām and our Dīn.

The Second Example

Allāmah Kaidānī[88] in his book *Khulāsatul Kaidānī* in the chapter Bāb al-Muḥaramāt (Chapter - On What is Unlawful) said,

> "Adding the word *Aᶜla* to the *takbīrs* and to say *Allāhu Akbar A'la* has not been transmitted from the The Messenger of Allāh (ﷺ) nor the companions (ﷺ)."

Now the word *Aᶜla* is an attribute of Allāh which means to be high or lofty, so what is the harm in saying this? Well simply because it is not established from the Messenger of Allāh (ﷺ) or the Salaf, therefore no one has permission to add the word *Aᶜla* to the *takbīrs* in the prayer.

[88] The book was written by Lutfallāh al-Naṣafi known as Fāẓıl Kaidānī who died in the 13/14th century. This book has continued to be taught in Ḥanafī Madāris, especially in the sub-continent for hundreds of years and is seen as a corner stone of basic Ḥanafī principals of Ṣalāh for the student. It is then very unfortunate that in it there are many errors. From amongst them is his saying: *"If someone does Rafᶜa al-Yadain, says Bismillāh loudly in the prayer, says Amīn loudly in the prayer and points his finger in the Tashahud, then all of these affairs are from those which are ḥarām i.e. unlawful" (ie invalidate the prayer.)* [*Khulāsatul Kaidānī* [pp.15-16]. Allāh's aid is sought as all the actions the author calls ḥarām are in fact established Sunnahs of the Messenger of Allāh (ﷺ)! This is the bigoted blind following found in books which are spoon fed to the Ḥanafī student so how can one expect that the student will have love for striving to reach the Sunnah of the Messenger of Allāh (ﷺ)?

Furthermore, the jurists also declared it unlawful (Ḥarām) to add these words. We have thus shown even if something is considered to be good and virtuous it cannot be understood to be correct, authentic and permissible if the words do not conform to the teachings and practices of the Messenger of Allāh (ﷺ).

The Fourth Doubt - *Tabarruk*[89]

Another doubt is presented which is concerning *tabarruk* ie seeking blessing. Numerous innovations and practices have been introduced under this false guise of *tabarruk*.

[89] Tabarruk means to seek blessing in or from something. [Ibn Athīr, *al-Nihāyah Fī Gharīb al-Ḥadīth* [1:120], al-Judaīᶜ, *al-Tabarruk Anwāᶜahu Wa Aḥkāmuhu* [p.30]. This is only restricted to the Prophets. Following the Sunnah and seeking blessing thereof is also a form of tabarruk. There is no Sharīᶜah proof to show that anyone besides the Messenger of Allāh (ﷺ) has the same position as him with respect to seeking tabarruk from the physical parts of his body. What has been said by al-Shāṭibī in *al-Eiᶜtisām* [2:6-7], *"The Prophet (ﷺ) never left anyone after himself anyone more superior than Abū Bakr as-Siddiq (رضي الله عنه), since he was his Khalīfah and no one did this through him... and nor through ᶜUmar (رضي الله عنه) and he was the best of the Ummah after him. Then likewise, Uthmān (رضي الله عنه) and then all of the Companions, with respect to whom there is no one who is more superior. There is not established from a single one of them any authentic report that states that someone would make tabarruk from them in any of these ways or what is similar to them. Rather they restricted themselves to following and imitating the actions and statements in which they (the Companions) followed the Prophet (ﷺ) This, therefore is a unanimous agreement from them for the abandonment of these things."* As for tabarruk through the righteous then this is by means of their righteous actions. Among the effects of this barakah of action of theirs is what good Allāh brings about on account of them and what harm He repels on account of them. **"And Your Lord would never destroy a township wrongfully, whilst its inhabitants are righteous." [Sūrah al-Hūd:117].** So this shows that the barakah of the righteous is in their actions and on account of their actions they bring about good for those besides them. As for making tabarruk through them, such as seeking to kiss their hands thinking that they contain physical barakah or touching them etc. then all of this is forbidden for anyone besides the Prophets. [Ṣāleh Āl ash-Shaikh, *Hadhihi Mafāhimūna* [pp.34-36].

Answer

Our position regarding *tabarruk* is also very plain and clear, a Muslim can only seek blessings or intend to receive reward from entities or things only the Messenger of Allāh (ﷺ) indicated, no one has the right to formulate anything they want as a source of blessing. Islamic principles have been overlooked and abandoned which lead to a wide array of obscure places of blessings being set up as businesses. The situation is as such, the masses begin to seek blessings and even prostrate whenever they see graves.[90] This tends to happen without them even investigating who is buried in the grave. Whenever they see a tree with a green or white flag, they run to seek blessings from it. Whenever they see a man wearing a long green gown with a long stick in his hand, with big rosary bead around his neck, they run to kiss his hand and feet to seek blessings.[91] Whereas, the fact of the matter is none of these people have anything that is blessed.

[90] One caller of modern times of the Sūfīs is Tāhir al-Qādirī who is the head of the callers to the gates of hell fire in Pākistān. He advocates openly that one should prostrate at the graves of the righteous in order to make tawassul and gain blessings. He has named such prostration as 'the prostration of veneration.' [refer to his book *al-Manhaj al-Sawī* [1:98], his book 'Istigātha Beseeching For Help and Lecture series entitled *'Tabarruk in Islām'*]. In fact, one can openly see on the web video sites that he allows his followers to prostrate to him openly!! Ibn Tayymīyah said, *"With regard to bowing when meeting, it is forbidden as it is narrated in al-Tirmidhī that they asked the Messenger of Allāh (ﷺ) about a man who meets his brother and bows to him. He said: "No, because it is not permissible to bow or prostrate to anyone except Allāh, may He be glorified. That may have been done by way of greeting under a law other than ours, as in the story of Yūsuf –* ***"...and they fell down before him prostrate. And he said: "O my father! This is the interpretation of my dream a foretime!" [Yūsuf:100].*** *But in our Sharīᶜah it is not permissible to prostrate to anyone except Allāh. Indeed, it is forbidden to stand as the Persians used to stand for one another – so what about bowing and prostrating? And a slight bow (as opposed to the full bow as in prayer) is also included in this prohibition."* [Ibn Taymiyyah, *Majmūᶜa al-Fatāwa* [1:377]. This evil caller has even been shunned by his own fellow Sūfī's and Barailwī's which should show the reader the depth of his misguidance. Our Shaikh, Maḥmūd Aḥmad Mirpūrī also reprimanded him. [Cf. Benefical Advice to Dr. Ṭāhir al-Qādirī, *Talkh Wa Shīrī* [pp.309-311]

[91] Ṭāhir al-Qādirī justifies the people prostrating to him on his website by saying that 'they were just trying to kiss his hands and feet'. This is the way the people of *shirk*

It is important to note here, not every individual can claim to do miracles and *karāmāt*[92] based on the miracles of the Messenger of Allāh (ﷺ). The *karāmāt* of the righteous people of Allāh are true,[93] however the righteous *Awliyā* will never claim any *karāmāt*. They supplicate to Allāh and at times a *karāmah* may take place. The true *Walī* will never claim he can double your wealth or give you daughters or sons. Likewise, he will not claim he can give you a special solution for your love live or enchanting amulets for that matter, rather, we find the Awliyā of Allāh supplicate and invoke Allāh with sheer humility.[94]

and *bidᶜah* interpret their actions when they are caught red handed defying the laws of Allāh. **"Except those who repent and do righteous deeds, and openly declare (the truth which they concealed). These, I will accept their repentance. And I am the One Who accepts repentance, the Most Merciful." [al-Baqarah:159]**

[92] Karāmah is: something exceptional which Allāh causes to occur at the hands of the righteous followers of Sunnah – as an honour from Allāh and as a blessing.' al-Fawzān said, *"A group has exaggerated in affirming the Karāmāt. This group has claimed Karāmāt for the magicians, swindlers and liars from the Shaikhs of the Sufis – to the extent that they worshiped them instead of Allāh – whether they are alive or dead. They have built structures upon the graves of those who claim Wilāya by narrating fabricated stories and attributing the power to manage the world and fulfil the need of those who call upon them and seek help from them. They call such people Aqtab (sing. Qutb) and Aghwath (sing. Gawth) due to these alleged Karāmāt and false stories. They have made this claim of Karāmāt a pretext to worship the one whom the Karāmah is attributed to. They call swindling, lying and magic a Karāmah perhaps because they do not distinguish between Karāmah and shaytanic acts. They do not differentiate between the Awliyā of the Rahman (i.e. Allāh) and Awliyā of the Shayṭān. Otherwise, it is known from the Qur'ān and the Sunnah that even if a certain person is proven to be Wali of Allāh and even if a Karāmah is caused to occur at his hands – it is not permissible to worship him instead of Allāh or seek* blessings from him or from his grave because worship is the Right of Allāh alone." [al-Fawzān, *Karāmāt al-Awliyā* [p.3]

[93] There is yet another hideous and slanderous accusation levied against the Salafī's and the Ahl al-Ḥadīth in that they reject the Karāmāt of the Awliyā! This is indeed a fallacious lie and the widest stretch of the imagination in order to belittle the Ahl al-Ḥadīth wa Ahl al-Sunnah.The Salaf and our revered scholars and Imāms in their own right authored numerous books and explained this basic Islamic precept in the wide array of books on ᶜAqīdah and Uṣūl.[Cf. Lālikā'ī, *Karāmāt al-Awliyā*, al-Khallāl, *Karāmāt al-Awliyā*, Ibn Taymiyyah, *al-ᶜAqīdah al-Wāsiṭīyyah* and Shāh Waliullāh's, *Tuḥfa al-Muwaḥḥidīn*]

[94] al-Fawzān said, *"So it has become clear that there is a difference between the Karāmāt of Awliyā and clowning of the swindlers and the liars which distinguishes*

All of the companions were the Wālīs of Allāh and the four rightly guided *Khulafā* and the ten (10) who were promised paradise, who have a lofty status. We find no examples or instances from their lives that people would seek blessing from them, or whether people went to their houses or graves after their deaths in order to seek blessing. All of these innovations were formulated in latter times and the *ᶜAqīdah* of seeking blessing from trees, stones, metal meshes around graves and soil is totally incorrect and baseless. No entity, whether it is a tree, stone or earth at any place can be blessed or virtuous until there is an authentic chain from the Messenger of Allāh (ﷺ) proving it is sacred, no matter how many good personalities and memories are associated with them. It is imperative to note the statement of ᶜUmar (رضي الله عنه) who

the truth from falsehood. The true Auliyā of Allāh do not use the Karāmāt - which Allāh causes to occur at their hands – to achieve position, deception and lower the eyes of the people in their honour Rather the Karāmāt of the Awliyā increases them in their humbleness and love for Allāh and seeking closeness to Allāh by worshiping him – as opposed to these swindlers and liars, who use these unusual Shaytanic acts to cause people to honour them, to come close to them and worship them instead of Allāh - until each one of these swindlers have a particular Tarīqah (way) and Jamāᶜah (group) which is named after him like the Shāḍhilīyyah, ar-Rifāᶜīyah, an-Naqshbandīyyah... and other Sūfī Tarīqah (way). The people are divided into three groups with regards to the issue of the Karāmāt. The first group exaggerated in denying the Karāmāt of the Awliyā until they rejected what is established in the Book and the Sunnah from the true Karāmāt that is caused (to occur by Allāh) for the righteous Awliyā of Allāh. The second group exaggerated in affirming the Karāmāt to the extent that they believed that magic, swindling and other deceptive acts are Karāmāt. They capitalized on this belief and made it a means of committing shirk and clinging to those who perform such unusual acts – whether they were dead or alive – until major shirk stemmed from it through worshiping the graves, and venerating the people and exaggeration in them when it was alleged that they possessed Karāmāt. The third group is Ahl al-Sunnah waᶜl-Jamāᶜah, which has an intermediate position which is free from exaggeration and shortcoming in affirming the Karāmāt. They affirm what is affirmed in the Qurʾān and the Sunnah. They neither exaggerate in (honouring) those who possess Karāmāt nor cling to them instead of Allāh, and they do not hold them superior to others. (because of their belief) that there might be Awliyā of Allāh who are superior to them although no Karāmah is caused to occur (by Allāh) at their hands. They also negate that which contradicts the Qurʾān and the Sunnah such as swindling and deception. They believe that this is from Shayṭān and are not Karāmāt of the Auliyā" [al-Fawzān, *Karāmāt al-Awliyā* [pp.6-7]. Cf. Ibn Taymiyyah, *al-ᶜAqīdah al-Wāsiṭīyyah* [pp.29-30] SRI Edn.

saidwhilst performing tawaf of the *Ka^cba* and he addressed the Black Stone and said,

"I know that you are a stone..."[95]

The people who fear trees, leaves, branches or anything slightly raised from the ground should take heed from this statement of ^cUmar (⁙) It should be also be noted, kissing and touching the Black Stone is a Sunnah of the Messenger of Allāh (⁙) and the only reason this has any significance and importance is because the Messenger of Allāh (⁙) would touch it otherwise the stone does not have any specific benefit that it can do anything. This is why ^cUmar (⁙) openly clarified this belief so that no one falls into error.

When this is the position regarding the Black Stone what significance does any other stone or religious artefact have, which some people have taken as items of blessing and virtue? What beliefs have we formulated with regards to trees, stones and other religious artefacts which the Messenger of Allāh (⁙) did not allude to. We have concocted our own virtues for certain religious artefacts for example by saying soil from a certain place has such a virtue etc or the leaf from such a tree has such and such a virtue and the meshwork from so and so grave has such and such blessing etc. All of these things are self concocted and fabrications and we say the only religious artefacts

---

[95] *al-Bukhārī* reports that ^cUmar (⁙) – came to the Black Stone (performing Tawāf, circumambulation), kissed it, and said, *"I know that you are a stone, you do not cause benefit or harm; and if it were not that I had seen Allāh's Messenger* Messenger of Allāh (⁙) *– kiss you, I would never have kissed you."* [*Bukhārī* [no.1520].
Reward of Kissing and Touching Black Stone.
[A] It was narrated that Ibn ^cUmar (⁙) said, I heard the Messenger of Allāh (⁙) say: *"Touching them both [the Black Stone and al-Rukn al-Yamāni] is an expiation for sins."* [*al-Tirmidhī* [no.959. This Ḥadīth was classed as Ḥasan by al-Tirmidhī and as Ṣaḥīḥ by *al-Hākim* (1:664). al-Dhahabī agreed with him]. [B] It was narrated that Ibn^cAbbās (⁙) said, The Messenger of Allāh (⁙) said concerning the Stone, *"By Allāh, Allāh will bring it forth on the Day of Resurrection, and it will have two eyes with which it will see and a tongue with which it will speak, and it will testify in favour of those who touched it in sincerity."* [al-*Tirmidhī,* [no.961], Ibn Mājah [no.2944]. This ḥadīth was classed as Ḥasan by al-Tirmidhī, and as strong by Ibn Ḥajr in *Fatḥ al-Bārī* [3:462]

which are blessed are those which the Messenger of Allāh (ﷺ) declared to be blessed.

Another common argument is put forward, that specific sacred incidences occurred at certain places or similarly a righteous or holy individual resided or visited a particular place. Therefore, such places must have some importance at the very least. In this regard we shall present one example which should suffice in rebutting and clarifying this doubt.

During the battle of Hudaibīyyah the Messenger of Allāh (ﷺ) took an oath of allegiance from his companions under a tree which became well known as the *Bay'ah Riḍwān*. This was an extremely important event because some of the most important individuals of this world were present with the best of mankind, Muhammad (ﷺ). Similarly, the world's most righteous individuals pledged their allegiance to him. An incident of this status that transpired under a tree truly blesses it and so if we were to debate and discuss what object alone associated with the Messenger of Allāh (ﷺ) constitutes being blessed then none can exceed this!

The people began visiting the tree frequently during the time of ᶜUmar (رضي الله عنه) in order see the revered site where a historical monumental event took place and due its tremendous status. We seek refuge in Allāh that it cannot be contemplated the companions intended to visit the tree in order to seek blessings from it. Despite this ᶜUmar (رضي الله عنه) removed the tree-only intending to curb something that could have unnecessarily spiralled out control.[96]

[96] Narrated by Nāfᶜe that, *ᶜUmar ibn al-Khaṭṭāb ordered the cutting of the tree under which the Messenger of Allāh (ﷺ) was pledged allegiance. He ordered for it to be cut' [as the people would go and pray under it, so he feared temptation for them].* [Ibn Waḍḍah, *Kitāb al-Bidᶜah*, Abū Bakr Ibn Abī Shaybah, *Muṣannaf Ibn Abī Shaybah* [no.7545]. Similarly, the Messenger of Allāh (ﷺ) destroyed any possible roots leading to *shirk* with Allāh. He was the most cautious when it came to tabarruk from objects which was not permissible. Abū Wāqid al-Laithī, *"We went out with the Messenger of Allāh (ﷺ) on the campaign to Hunain while we had just left disbelief (kufr) for Islām. The pagans had a sidrah (lote-tree) called Dhāt Anwāṭ where they would remain and hang their arms upon it. When we passed by it we said, 'O Messenger of Allāh, won't you make for us another Dhāt Anwāṭ just like their Dhāt Anwāṭ? The Messenger of Allāh said, Allāhu Akbar! By the One in Whose Hand is my soul, verily these are the ways of the earlier nations. You have said exactly as the Banū Isrāil have said to*

He feared the future generation would go to extremes in revering the tree and err into thinking the tree was virtuous and that it's leaves, branches and roots were a means of blessing. Furthermore, So in order to prevent the tree from becoming a historic monument and something that would lead to and become a means of *shirk*, ʿUmar (⸎) uprooted the tree, so people with weak ʿAqīdah in future generations do not fall into *shirk* and innovations.

We ask the people, to sincerely ponder and tell us whether ʿUmar bin al-Khaṭṭāb (⸎) was a Wahhābī? We seek refuge in Allāh from such a thought and that is, did he (ie ʿUmar) intend to degrade or demote the Messenger of Allāh (ﷺ)?

Absolutely not, having such thoughts about the great ʿUmar al-Farūq (⸎) is clear ignorance. This is however, a real life historical event, which nobody can deny this clear reality. Why are we setting up places everywhere to in order to seek blessings from them? The issue of *ʿAqīdah* is very important and highly intricate and thus, one must traverse it with sincerity and a calm mind, which may lead him to a greater understanding.

The Fifth Doubt – The Practice of the Companions

The people attempt to present another doubt, they say if every new thing in the Dīn is an innovation- why did the companions do certain things during their era which were not practised during the life of the Messenger of Allāh (ﷺ), whereas those things are considered part of the Dīn now. For example, compiling and collating the Qurʾān,[97] the

Musa, "Make for us a god just as their Gods He (Mūsa) said, Verily you are an ignorant people (7:138)." Certainly, you will follow the ways of those who went before you." [*Tirmidhī* [no.2180] and it is Ṣaḥīḥ]. Muḥammad bin ʿAbdul Wahhāb comments on this ḥadīth saying that good intentions by themselves are not enough for deeds to be accepted and that the action must be in accordance with the Sunnah. [Muḥammad bin ʿAbdul Wahhāb, *Kitāb ut-Tawḥīd*, chapter 9].

[97] This is from amongst one of their biggest doubts presented but it is futile. In brief the answer to them is from many angles in why this action cannot be called a *bidʿah* and it is, **[A]** It is agreed by consensus of the Ummah that the Messenger of Allāh (ﷺ) had scribes during his lifetime who wrote down the Qurʾān so this cannot be a *bidʿah*.

second *Ādhān* for *Jumu^cah*, the *Tarāwīḥ* prayer[98] in congregation, explanations and translations of the Qur'ān. Hence, this shows good practices and customs can be introduced into Islām in our times!

Answer

Before we answer this doubt in detail whilst addressing every issue separately, it is important to clarify that if we accept this evidence of the people of innovation, ie there is no harm in doing something new in the Dīn or how can a good deed be labelled as an innovation? In answer, we would like to ask them a rhetorical question, if every apparent righteous action cannot be labelled as an innovation, then can you please tell what an innovation is then? Also the affairs the Messenger of Allāh (ﷺ) vehemently exerted great effort in warning us about, which have been called innovation, what exactly are they then?

We will cite some aḥadīth in which the Messenger of Allāh (ﷺ) declared innovations to be dangerous for our Dīn and Imān. In such aḥadīth he also instructed us to beware of them. It should be borne in mind the Messenger of Allāh (ﷺ) has already declared fornication, alcohol, stealing, oppression and lying to be impermissible and unlawful, therefore what are innovations? We will summarise this point again later making it easy to understand this discussion.

The First Evidence

al-Irbād ibn Sāriyah (رضي الله عنه) narrates,

[B] Abū Bakr initiated the collection of all the Qur'ān as a single book and we have been commanded to follow his Sunnah and that of the rightly guided khulāfah, **[C]** Ibn Ḥajr states *"The Qur'ān was written at the time of the Messenger of Allāh (ﷺ) in various places but not compiled. Abu Bakr compiled in a book form and Uthmān made copies of it in his era"* [*Fatḥ al-Bāri* [9:10] **[D]** No companion called this action a *bid'ah* or even *'Bid'ah Ḥasanah'* a good *bid'ah*' and this in itself proves that the companions did not see this action as an innovation yet the Sūfi of today is adamant in making the compiling and writing of the Qur'ān a *bid'ah* so he can continue to fool the people and feed his belly through his *bid'ah*.

[98] These are explained by the Shaikh further in this treatise.

"The Messenger of Allāh (ﷺ) gave us an eloquent sermon one day after the early morning prayer due to which the eyes flowed with tears and the hearts were moved so one of us said, "Oh Messenger of Allāh, it is as if this is a farewell sermon so what do you advise us with?" He (ﷺ) said, "I advise you with the fear of Allāh and to hear and obey (your leaders) even if an Abyssinian slave were to rule over you for whomsoever lives amongst you after me then they will see many differences so beware of the newly invented matters for it is misguidance. So whoever reaches that amongst you then upon you is to follow my Sunnah and the Sunnah of the Rightly Guided Caliphs. Stick to it and bite onto it with the molar teeth." [Mishkāt Vol.1 Kitāb al-ᶜEi'tisām Bil-Kitāb Waᶜl Sunnah, Musnad Aḥmad, Abū Dāwūd, Tirmidhī][99]

The Second Evidence

Guḍaif bin al-Ḥārith (رضي الله عنه) narrates the Messenger of Allāh (ﷺ) said,

"Whenever a people introduce an innovation then something similar to it from the Sunnah is taken away-sticking to the Sunnah is better than innovating."(Musnad Ahmad)[100]

[99] Aḥmad, *Musnad* [4:46-47], *Abū Dāwūd* [no.4607], *al-Tirmidhī* [no.2676], *Ibn Mājah* [no's 42-44], Tirmidhī graded it Ḥasan Ṣaḥīḥ, al-Albānī graded it Ṣaḥīḥ in *Ṣaḥīḥ Sunan al-Tirmidhī* [3:69 no.2676], *Ṣaḥīḥ Sunan Abī Dāwūd* [3:118 no.4607], *Ṣaḥīḥ Sunan Ibn Mājah* [1:31 no.40-41] and further references it to *al-Irwā al-Ghalīl* [no.2455], *al-Mishkāt* [no.165], *al-Ẓilāl al-Jannah* [no's.26-34], *Ṣalah al-Tarāwīḥ* [no's.88-89]. Ibn Ḥajr, *Hidāyah ur-Rūwāh Ila Takhrīj Aḥadīth al-Maṣabīḥ Waᶜl Mishkāt* [1:130 no.164] with al-Albāni's verification, ᶜAlī Ḥasan al-Ḥalabī added the chain is authentic, Tirmidhī graded is Ḥasan Ṣaḥīḥ and a group authenticated it and from them is al-Ḍhiya al-Maqdisī in *'Ittibaᶜ as-Sunan Wa Ijtināb al-Bidᶜah'* [1:79] Manuscript]

[100] Aḥmad, *Musnad* (28:172 no.16970), al-Ṭabrīzī, *Mishkāt al-Maṣābīh* [1:66 no.187], Abū Hafs, al-Bazzār, *Musnad al-Bazzār* [no.131 with *Kashf Astār],* al-Lālikāᶜī, *Sharḥ Usūl al-Ei'tiqād* [1:102-121], Muḥammad Ibn Naṣr, *as-Sunnah* [p.32 no.97], Ibn Baṭṭah, al-Ibānah [1:224-248], Abū Shāmah, *al-Bā'ith ᶜA'la Inkār al-Bidᶜah Wal-Ḥawādith* [p.88], Ibn ᶜAsākir, *Tārīkh Dimishq* [14:137], al-Haithamī, *al-Majmᶜa az-Zawāʾid* [1:188 no.892]. Haithamī added, *"Narrated Aḥmad and Bazzār and the chain contains Abū Bakr ibn ᶜAbd Allāh bin Abī Maryam who is rejected in ḥadīth."* [al-Ṭabarānī, *Muᶜjam al-Kabīr* [18:99 no.178]. Ibn Ḥajr declared it Ḥasan in *Fatḥ ul-Bārī*

The Third Evidence

Ḥassān Ibn ᶜAṭīyyah said,

> "The nation that introduces an innovation into the Dīn, then Allāh will take away it's like from their Sunnah from them and it will not be returned to them until the day of judgement."[al-Dārimī][101]

The Fourth Evidence

Ibrāhīm bin Maīsarah said,

> "Whoever honours an innovator then verily he has aided the destruction of Islām."[102]

These narrations clarify the gravity and dangers of innovations.[103] Whatever the Messenger of Allāh (ﷺ) declared to be unlawful, the Qur'ān also declared it to be impermissible and unlawful, therefore there is no need to call them innovations. However, there are certain practices, which have been labelled as innovations, which are practised by the people because they think they are righteous deeds. In this regard even if the people added something into the Dīn from

[3:253]. Ibn al-Mundhir, *at-Targhīb Wat-Tarhīb* [1:45 no.83], al-Suyūṭī, *al-Jāmᶜe al-Saghīr* [2:480 no.7790], Shawkānī, *Nayl al-Awṭār* [3:333], who said, *"Its chain contains Ibn Abī Maryam who is weak and Baqīyyah who is a mudallis."* al-Albānī graded it weak in *Ḍaᶜīf at-Targīb* [1:10 no.37] and also in his *Silsilah Aḥadith al-Ḍaᶜīfah Wal-Mawdūᶜah* [14:454 no.6707]. Ubaidullāh Mubārakpūrī also declared it to be weak and discusses its variant routes in *Mirᶜah al-Mafātīh* [1:291 no.187]

[101] al-Dārimī, *Sunan* [1:35 no.98], Ibn al-Waḍḍah, *al-Bidᶜah* [2:80 no.90], Ibn Baṭṭah, *al-Ibānah* [1:351 no.228], Lālikāᶜī, *Sharḥ Usūl al-Eiᶜtiqād* [1:104 no.129], Abū Nuᶜaym, *al-Ḥilyah* [6:73]. al-Albānī graded it Ṣaḥīḥ (authentic) in *al-Mishkāt* [1:66 no.188]

[102] al-Lālikāᶜī, *Sharḥ Uṣūl al-ᶜEiᶜtiqād* [1:139 no.267], al-Tabrīzī, *Mishkāt al-Maṣābīh,* [1:189].

[103] The action of an innovator leads to the hatred for Islām. When an innovator acts on the evilness of his innovation it leads the enemy of Islām to hate and harbour rancour against Islām whereas Islām is totally free from all of these innovations. [Ṣāleḥ Ibn Saᶜd al-Suḥaimī, *Tanbīyyah Ulil al-Abṣār* [p.195].

themselves thinking they were virtuous or praiseworthy, they would still be unacceptable and in fact they would be rejected. Hence, innovations have no place in the Dīn. We will cite two more aḥadīth which further clarify this issue in greater detail.

Evidence from the Aḥadith
The First Ḥadīth

It was narrated by Anas bin Mālik (⚬) who said,

"A group of three men came to the houses of the wives of the Messenger of Allāh (⚬) asking how the Messenger of Allāh (⚬) worshipped (Allāh), and when they were informed about that, they considered their worship insufficient and said, "Where are we compared to the Messenger of Allāh (⚬) as his past and future sins have been forgiven." Then one of them said, "I will offer the prayer throughout the night forever." The other said, "I will fast throughout the year and will not break my fast." The third said, "I will keep away from the women and will not marry forever." Allāh's Apostle came to them and said, "Are you the same people who said so-and-so? By Allāh, I am more submissive to Allāh and more afraid of Him than you; yet I fast and break my fast, I do sleep and I also marry women. So he who does not follow my tradition in religion, is not from me (not one of my followers)." [Bukhārī, Muslim][104]

The Second Ḥadīth

al-Dārimī transmits that Abū Mūsa al-Ashʿarī (⚬) said,

"We used to sit by the door of ʿAbd Allāh ibn Masʿūd before the Morning Prayer, so that when he came out we would walk with him to the mosque. (One day) Abū Mūsa al-Ashʿarī came to us and said: "Has Abūʿ Abdal-Rahman come out yet?" We replied No. So he sat down with us until he came out. When he came out, we all stood along with him, so Abū Mūsa said to him: "O Abū ʿAbdal-Rahman! I have just seen something in the

---

104 Bukhārī [no.5063], Muslim [no.1401]

mosque which I considered wrong, but all praise is for Allāh, I did not see anything except good in it." He inquired: "What is it?" Abū Mūsa replied: "If you live you will see it. I saw in the mosque people sitting in circles awaiting the Prayer. In each circle they had pebbles in their hands and a man would say: Repeat Allāhu Akbar a hundred times. So they would repeat it a hundred times. Then he would say: say La Ilaha illAllāh a hundred times. So they would say it a hundred times. Then he would say: say SubhanAllāh a hundred times. So they would say it a hundred times." Ibn Masᶜūd asked: "What did you say to them?" Abū Mūsā said: "I did not say anything to them. Instead I waited to hear your view on it." Ibn Masᶜūd replied: "Would that you had ordered them to count their evil deeds and assured them that their good deeds would not be lost!" Then we went along with him until he came to one of these circles whereby he stood and said: "What is this I see you doing?" They replied: "O Abū ᶜAbdal-Rahmān! These are pebbles upon which we are counting takbīr, tahlīl and tasbīh." He said: "Count your evil deeds instead. I assure you that none of your good deeds will be lost. Woe to you, O Ummah of Muḥammad (ﷺ), how quickly you go to destruction! Here are your Prophet's Companions available in abundance (mutawafirun). And there are his clothes which have not yet decayed and his bowl which is unbroken. By Him in Whose Hand is my soul! Either you are following a Religion that is better guided than the Religion of Muhammad (ﷺ) or you are opening a door of misguidance." They said: "O Abu `Abd al-Rahman! By Allāh, we only intend good!" He said: "How many are there who intend good but do not achieve it. Indeed Allāh's Messenger (ﷺ) said to us: A people will recite the Qur'an but it will not pass beyond their throats. By Allāh! I do not know, but perhaps most of them are from among you." Then he left them. Amar bin Salima said: We saw most of those people fighting against us on the day of Nahrawān, on the side of the Khawārij. [Sunan al-Dārimī][105]

Dear readers, read both narrations very carefully again and then decide why practising these righteous actions were prohibited. The Messenger of Allāh (ﷺ) himself forbade one of them and the illustrious companion vehemently warned against the other. The reality of innovations becomes very clear after reading these narrations.

[105] al-Dārimī, *as-Sunan* [1:48-49 no.204], in the Muqaddimah from al-Ḥakam ibn al-Mubārak who narrates from ᶜUmar bin Yaḥya who narrates from his father Yaḥya who narrates from ᶜAmar bin Sālima. See a previous footnotes for further explanation of this narration.

Now we will have a look at why the companions performed certain actions, which the people of innovation use as evidence. These were raised under the subheading of the fifth doubt. We have already clarified the Qur'ān and Sunnah mention actions, which are lawful, unlawful, prohibited and abandoned actions; therefore, there is no need to call them innovations. Innovations are actions or practices, which appear to be good and virtuous, and the people who practice them believe they are righteous deeds and hence rewarding. However furthermore, they (ie the innovations) have no evidence or basis in the Sharīᶜah neither is there a need for them to be practised.

In this regard, before we progress into answering the doubts raised by the people of innovation in detail, it is necessary to clarify an important point and that is, any action a human does, he does so for a worldly or religious reason. If the action is pertaining to this world in order to gain some luxury and comfort, for example travelling by car, then it is well known there were no cars[106] during the life of the Messenger of Allāh (ﷺ). Yet we know the Messenger of Allāh (ﷺ) did travel and he used whatever means of travel were available to him, for example horses, camels and donkeys. Undoubtedly, the car was invented much later and a quicker way to travel, hence it is permissible because Messenger of Allāh (ﷺ) would use the fastest ride available to him. However, if anything new that opposes the Qur'ān and Sunnah will be deemed impermissible. We have the example of business transactions, any lawful form of business can be utilised however if it involves usury it will be unlawful because riba has been clearly declared to be unlawful in the Qur'ān and Sunnah.

The second element is concerning actions, which are performed with regards to the Dīn, we must look for evidences for them in the Qur'ān and Sunnah, whether they are established from the companions or from any examples of the ijtihad of the jurists.[107] If there are

[106] See above footnotes concerning *bidᶜah* in the Dīn and the Dunyā.

[107] Ijtihād which is derived from the Qur'ān and Sunnah is accepted and one which is based on merely opinion can be accepted or left as this does not form part of the legislation. Ibn Qayyīm has written extensively on the rules and regulations concerning Ijtihād and that it must be based on the sources of the Dīn [Qur'ān, Sunnah,

evidences from the aforementioned methods for any action or practise, there is no problem and we may proceed with the action because it is permissible.[108]

In this regard, the reason why an action is being practised will be looked at, meaning was there a reason to perform the action during the time of the Messenger of Allāh (ﷺ) and the companions. If the reason was present during their times, the restriction that prevented the Messenger of Allāh (ﷺ) and the companions from performing the action needs to be looked at. Hence, if the reason to perform the action was present without any restrictions during the time of the Messenger of Allāh (ﷺ) and the companions, yet despite all this, the action was not performed nor did a new reason arise for the action to be performed; but an individual persists in performing the action, thinking it to be part of the Dīn, then there is no doubt in the action being an innovation. If this principle is understood and applied to the situations we face, then all of the allegations and doubts presented by the people of innovation will be answered very easily and succinctly.[109]

For example, we have often seen the customary practice after the funeral prayer, as soon as it finishes the Imām instructs everyone to recite *Sūrah Fātiḥah* a certain number of times and to recite *Sūrah Ikhlās* a certain number of times etc. It seems apparent the intent of this is for the deceased to gain reward and for him to be forgiven. So reciting *Sūrah Fātiḥah* and *Sūrah Ikhlās* in this specific method and time has no basis or any evidence whatsoever from the Qurʾān or

Ijmā and al-Qiyās al-Sharᶜī] rather than pure analogy and opinion in his book *'Iᶜlām al-Muwaqqᶜīn'* [1:165-172].

[108] Cf. The chapter on Ṣalah al-Janāzah [Maḥmūd Aḥmad Mirpūrī, *Fatāwa Ṣirāt al-Mustaqīm* [pp.240-268]

[109] Numerous scholars have authored books refuting the people of innovation and their false principles which oppose the pristine Sunnah. They include *Kitāb Fīhi Mā Jā' Fi'l Bidāh* of Ibn Waḍāḥ (d.900/287), *al-Rad ᶜAla Ahl al-Bidᶜah wa Tabyīn Uṣūl al-Sunnah* of Abi'l Qāsim Maslamah bin al-Qāsim al-Qurṭubī (d.964/353), *Kitāb al-Ḥawādith Wa'l Bidāh* of Ṭarṭūshī (d.1081/474), *al-Bā'ith ᶜA'la Inkār al-Bidᶜah Wal-Ḥawādith* of Abū Shāmah (d.1267/665) and numerous others.

Ḥadīth and nor did any of the companions practise this neither did the four Imāms for that matter.[110]

We then look at the reason why this practise was formulated, it was for the deceased to gain reward and for him to be ultimately forgiven. However, people also died during the time of the Messenger of Allāh (ﷺ) including his companions, this form of seeking forgiveness and attaining reward for the deceased was something they could have practised, but despite this, they did not. We find they sufficed with the prescribed supplications and invocations in the funeral prayer. Furthermore, nothing prevented them from performing such actions during their times and therefore the reasons which are mentioned for performing such actions are null and void.

The method of praying the funeral of a Muslim is well known and established, so undoubtedly this is an attempt to introduce something new into the Dīn. Such innovations become a burden for the people without any reward or forgiveness. Therefore, it is mandatory to abstain from such innovations.

The people of innovation hide behind another principle of the Sharīᶜah which they often use. They say, we have been commanded to perform certain actions and to abstain from others. Yet there are actions that have no clear rulings,[111] therefore such actions are mubah ie permissible and therefore they cannot be innovations. We say using this deduction and reasoning by the people of innovation is synonymous in deceiving themselves. If we were to accept this principle of the people of innovation, it still poses further problems and more questions. When an individual decides to perform an action based on its permissibility, who has the authority to define and decide

[110] See above footnotes on how *bidᶜah* continues to change and has many variations whilst the Sunnah and its methodology of performance, frequency, timing etc. are all stipulated by the Messenger of Allāh (ﷺ) himself.

[111] See above note concerning the discussion on 'Mubāh' and the differentiation between that which is permissible in the Dīn must require a text. al-Shāṭibī said, *"That which is from the affairs of the Dīn is by its foundation is impermissible unless there is a text to prove otherwise"* [al-Shāṭibī, *al-Eiᶜtisām* [1:176]. Ibn Taymiyyah stated that, *"Imām Aḥmad Ibn Ḥanbal and other Ahl al-Ḥadīth say that all that which is ᶜIbādah [Dīn] is forbidden unless a text shows otherwise as the legislator is Allāh alone."* [Ibn Taymiyyah, *al-Majmūᶜa al-Fatāwa* [18:29]

the methods of that action. Thus the question arises, under what basis will these people introduce these new actions?

Let us take the example we mentioned previously, a person prays the funeral prayer and then argues, because there is nothing established from the Messenger of Allāh (ﷺ) as to what should recited before or after the prayer, so anything we recite cannot be an innovation.[112] We ask, this new formulated method, which is conducted after the funeral prayer, lets, says for instance the people differ over the method and three groups arise. One group says recite Sūrah Fātiḥah and Sūrah Ikhlās 3 times the second group says to recite Sūrah Yāsin and then the third groups says to recite *Sūrah Fātiḥah* and the salutation. So now the contention is who will decide what the correct way is? It is often the case, the opinion of the majority of the people is accepted or the common practices of the masses are given precedence. So therefore attempting to decide what is permissible or impermissible generates more confusion, which eventually leads to the introduction of innovations into the Dīn.

Therefore, we have a very simple principle, whatever the Messenger of Allāh (ﷺ) did, we do and wherever he prohibited, we stop at that. Wherever he remained silent, we will remain silent-how peaceful and easy is this. The Messenger of Allāh (ﷺ) informed us of the method of performing the funeral prayer, how to the prepare graves, how to lower the deceased into the grave and the supplications he made thereafter, is this not sufficient for us? Therefore, the intent of the people of innovation and their deductions for what is mubah (ie permissible) is incorrect.

In this way, everyone can have a free and open choice to introduce any innovation or practice, they can do this whenever they want and then present this as part of the Dīn. In fact, mubah refers to affairs which have not been specifically identified with clear rulings, there is scope for opinions based on *ijtihād*, analytical deductions, elucidations and authentic analogical reasoning. How does this prove we have the

[112] In this regard there are a number of authorative and beneficial works authored by the scholars of Ahl al-Ḥadīth with regards to the rulings pertaining to the funeral prayer. [Cf. ᶜAbdur Rahmān al-Mubārakpūrī's, *Aḥkām al-Janā'iz*, al-Albānī's, *Aḥkām al-Janā'iz wa Bidᶜauhā* and Muḥammad Raʾīs Nadwī's *Namāz Janāzah*.]

authority to introduce new actions and practices into established forms of worship?

Likewise, if there is a need to perform particular action at specific times they will not be understood to be forms of worship nor can a person enforce such actions. When the Messenger of Allāh (ﷺ) has already informed us of the permissible forms worship from the beginning till the end, nobody has any position or authority to innovate anything new in the Dīn. Examples of *ijtihād* and *Qiyās* are tools of Fiqh, which the Imāms and expert scholars of this Ummah utilised from the Qur'ān and Sunnah. In this era, the innovations and newly invented matters the people of innovation have introduced under the false guise of mubah and to accumulate wealth and luxury,[113] are not even remotely found in any of the books of Fiqh from any of the Imāms.

Other Doubts

They say Tarāwīḥ was never prayed in congregation during the time of the Messenger of Allāh (ﷺ) nor during the era of Abū Bakr as-Siddīque (رضي الله عنه) during the month of Ramaḍan.[114] ᶜUmar (رضي الله عنه) was the first person who started this prayer in congregation-and we seek refuge in Allāh that Umar (رضي الله عنه) innovated something new in the Dīn.[115]

[113] This is referring to the money the 'Pīrs' charge for writing Taᶜwīz and amulets, for their live TV Istikhārah sessions and for other such dubious and heinous practices. [Cf. The Taᶜwīz selling elders should fear Allāh [Maḥmūd Aḥmad Mirpūrī, *Talkh Wa Shīrī* [pp.65-68]

[114] This is yet another preposterous notion and an outrageously ignorant claim that they make and thus unsurprisingly it can only be made by the Ḥanafī muqallids. This has been undoubtedly answered by Shaikh Maḥmūd but let the delusional detractor refer to the book of Muḥammad Abu'l Qāsim Sayf Banārasī [d.1949/1368), *Husn al-Ṣanāᶜa Fī Ṣalāh al-Tarāwīḥ Bi'l Jamāᶜah* wherein he overwhelming proves Tarāwīḥ was prayed in Jamāᶜah. It also shows this claim of the muqallidīn and the people of innovation is an old argument and bearing in mind Muḥammad Abu'l Qāsim Sayf Banārasī was born in (b.1889/1306) meaning this reckless claim by the despondents was most probably answered over a 100 years ago.

[115] The doubt Shaikh Maḥmūd Aḥmad Mirpūrī is answering here is raised by the people of innovation from the following ḥadīth, that *"ᶜAbdur Rahmān bin ᶜAbdul Qārī*

The First Principle

Is to remember here is that any ijtihād or an action of a companion which is not opposed by any other companions is permissible without any difference of opinion. The Messenger of Allāh (ﷺ) himself commanded us to follow the way of the companions and their example. He further vehemently instructed us to follow the way of the rightly guided *Khulāfa* which has been transmitted in the authentic Ḥadīth

> "Hold firmly onto my Sunnah and the Sunnah of my rightly guided Khulāfa."[116]

So not only is this action of ᶜUmar (رضي الله عنه) acceptable but rather it is also the Sunnah.[117]

The Second Principle

The actions of ᶜUmar (رضي الله عنه) were not new assuming there was no evidence from the Messenger of Allāh (ﷺ), whereas in fact it is clearly established the Messenger of Allāh (ﷺ) prayed *Tarāwīḥ* in

said, "I went out in the company of ᶜUmar bin al-Khaṭṭāb one night in Ramaḍan to the mosque and found the people praying in different groups. A man praying alone or a man praying with a little group behind him. So, ᶜUmar said, 'In my opinion I would better collect these (people) under the leadership of one Qārī (Reciter) (i.e. let them pray in congregation!)'. So, he made up his mind to congregate them behind ᶜUbay bin Kaᶜb. Then on another night I went again in his company and the people were praying behind their reciter. On that, ᶜUmar remarked, 'What an excellent bidᶜah (نِعْمَ الْبِدْعَةُ هَذِهِ) i.e. innovation in religion) this is; but the prayer which they do not perform, but sleep at its time is better than the one they are offering.' He meant the prayer in the last part of the night. (In those days) people used to pray in the early part of the night." [*Bukhārī* [no.2010]

116 See the Ḥadīth of ᶜIrbād Ibn Sāriyah (رضي الله عنه) which has preceded.

117 The Messenger of Allāh (ﷺ) instructed us to follow and obey his rightly guided Khulafā and thus is from the Sunnah of the rightly guided Khulafā [Ibn Rajab, *Jāmᶜe al-Ulūm al-Hikam* [2:129]

congregation for 3 days.[118] Therefore, the Messenger of Allāh (ﷺ) praying *Tarāwīḥ* for three (3) days established its permissibility himself. We know innovations do not have any basis in the Dīn whatsoever, whereas the basis to pray Tarāwīḥ in congregation does exist.

The Third Principle

The reason ᶜUmar (رضي الله عنه) gathered the people to pray collectively in Jamāᶜah was when he saw them praying individually or in smaller congregations, which demonstrated differing and splitting. Thus in order to prevent them from being disunited he sensed the need to unite everyone, he instructed them to pray as one united body in the worship of Allāh.

This was the reason why he instructed them to pray in congregation. If they argue[119] and say the cause of this splitting and disunity also existed during the time of the Messenger of Allāh (ﷺ). Then we say this is correct and the same cause actually did exist but prior to this we also mentioned another principle, if there is reason to practice a new action but there are restrictions at the time, which essentially prohibit or prevent the action from being performed and

[118] The evidence for this is the Ḥadīth of Abū Dharr (رضي الله عنه) said, *"We kept the fasts of Ramaḍhān with the Messenger of Allāh (ﷺ), then he led us in Qīyām (Tarāwīḥ prayer) on the 23rd night (when seven nights were left) till about one third of it passed. He did not observe it on the 24th, then on the 25th night he led us till about half the night passed. We requested to offer supererogatory prayer during the whole night. The Messenger of Allāh (ﷺ) said, "He who observes Qīyām along with the Imām till he finishes it, then it is as if he offered prayer the whole night." Then he did not observe the Qīyām with us on the 26th night, then finally on the 27th night he gathered his wives, members of his household and the people and he led everyone in the Qīyām (Tarāwīḥ prayer) till we feared of missing the dawn meal."* [*Ibn Mājah* [2:287 no.1327] *Ṣaḥīḥ Ibn Mājah* [[1:395 no.1344 and no.1100] according to the numbering of al-Albānī, *Abī Dāwūd* [1:217 no.1245], *Tirmidhī* [1:72-73], *Ṣaḥīḥ Nasāᶜī* [1:338], *Muṣannaf Ibn Abī Shaybah* [2:90 no.21), *Sharḥ Māᶜanī al-Āthār* [1:206), Muḥammad Ibn Nāsr al-Marwazī, *Qīyām al-Layl* [p.89], *al-Faryābī* [2:71-72], *Baihaqī* [2:294], al-Albānī, *Irwā* [no.447], *Mishkāt* [no.1298], *Ṣalāh al-Tarāwīḥ* [pp.16-17]. al-Albānī said Ṣaḥīḥ, Nimawī, *Āthār as-Sunan* [p.347], Ẓafar Aḥmad Thanwī, *Eᶜlā as-Sunan* [7:38].

[119] The claimants and advocators of innovations ie the innovators.

thus it was not practised at that particular time. Thereafter, when the restricting and or preventative factors are eliminated, the practise of that particular action becomes permissible. Therefore, there was a preventative or restrictive reason during the time of the Messenger of Allāh (ﷺ) which prohibited praying *Tarāwīḥ* regularly in congregation during the life. The Messenger of Allāh (ﷺ) informed us of this himself via the narration of Zaid bin Thābit (رضي الله عنه) where he narrates,

> "Allāh's Messenger (ﷺ) made a small room (with a palm leaf mat). Allāh's Messenger (ﷺ) came out (of his house) and prayed in it. Some men came and joined him in his prayer. Then again the next night they came for the prayer, but Allāh's Messenger (ﷺ) delayed and did not come out to them. So they raised their voices and knocked the door with small stones (to draw his attention). He came out to them in a state of anger, saying, "You are still insisting (on your deed, i.e. Tarāwīḥ prayer in the mosque) that I thought that this prayer (Tarāwīḥ) might become obligatory on you. So you people, offer this prayer at your homes, for the best prayer of a person is the one which he offers at home, except the compulsory (congregational) prayer." (Bukhārī, Muslim)[120]

We clearly find from this Ḥadīth, the main concern of the Messenger of Allāh (ﷺ) was the fear of this prayer becoming obligatory-this was the preventative and restrictive measure as well as the reason the Messenger of Allāh (ﷺ) did not pray with the congregation in the nights that followed. The restriction was fear of the prayer becoming obligatory and thus was the restrictive factor; however, this was only the case when the *Sharīcah* was being revealed.

During the time of cUmar (رضي الله عنه) this preventative measure was void because revelations had stopped[121] and the possibility of praying in congregation becoming obligatory was impossible and obsolete. So therefore, he gathered the people and instructed them to pray in congregation, which the Messenger of Allāh (ﷺ) had already previously done. It is at this instance he said this is a good new thing ie a good *bidcah*. So cUmar (رضي الله عنه) did not start anything new which had no basis in the Dīn; therefore, saying cUmar (رضي الله عنه) started an innovation

[120] *Bukhārī* [no.6113]. The wording of this Ḥadīth is also supported by the Ḥadīth of Ācishah (رضي الله عنها), Cf. *Bukhārī* [no.1129], *Muslim* [no.761]
[121] Hence the prayer could no longer be made obligatory as revelations had stopped.

is sheer ignorance and a clear evidence of a deficient understanding of the principles ie the Uṣūl of the Dīn.

Another doubt they often cast is concerning the *Ādhān* for *Jumu*ᶜ*ah* during the time of the Messenger of Allāh (ﷺ) and then Uthmān (رضي الله عنه) introduced the second Ādhān, therefore is this also an innovation (ie a *bid*ᶜ*ah*)?

We have already previously mentioned, the new affairs the companions and especially the rightly guided *Khulafā* introduced based on the *ijtihād* they performed with regards to the necessary affairs of the Dīn which were relevant to their times, are not only permissible but are in fact also recommended. Furthermore, such affairs, which not even a single companion opposed which essentially and almost equates to an *Ijmā*ᶜ.[122]

Furthermore, Uthmān (رضي الله عنه) did not start anything new for which there was no basis in the Dīn, because calling the Ādhān for Jumuᶜah was already implemented and established. Thereafter a reason or a need arose during the time of Uthmān (رضي الله عنه), that the people became lax and lenient so he introduced the second *Ādhān* in order to remind the ever-expanding community to prepare for the Friday prayer. The *Ādhān* would be called and projected loudly outside the masjid to serve as a reminder.

It is also important and necessary to clarify another issue here and that is, whoever upholds and follows the way of the Messenger of Allāh (ﷺ) and calls the *Ādhān* only once, then, not only is this permissible but it also better according to some scholars.

[122] This form of Ijmāᶜ is known as Ijmāᶜ Sukūti, ie silence indicating unanimous agreement without any opposition. This particular issue is vast and expansive and well out of the remit of this treatise because of the intricacies and specific minute technicalities between the Uṣūli scholars. This particular deduction of Shaikh Maḥmūd Aḥmad Mirpūrī has eminent value because of the agreed understanding of what exactly constitutes an Ijmāᶜ and what is closest to the truth insha'Allāh as it relayed from Aḥmed bin Ḥanbal and others. This was expounded by the Andalūsian Jurist, Zahirite and Ḥadīth Master, Ibn Ḥazm in his *'al-Iḥkām Fī Uṣūl al-Aḥkām'* [4:538+] and his acclaimed but succinct summary *'an-Nubḍ Fī Uṣūl al-Fiqh'* [pp.15+] wherein he also discusses and debates the variant opinions and concludes that Ijmᶜa or an unanimous collective agreement is only of the companions and anything claimed otherwise will not be free from error.